Understanding Company News

How to interpret stock market announcements

Rodney Hobson

HARRIMAN HOUSE LTD

3A Penns Road
Petersfield
Hampshire
GU32 2EW
GREAT BRITAIN

Tel: +44 (0)1730 233870
Email: enquiries@harriman-house.com
Website: www.harriman-house.com

First published in Great Britain in 2010
Copyright © Harriman House Ltd

The right of Rodney Hobson to be identified as Author has been asserted in accordance with the Copyright, Design and Patents Act 1988.

ISBN: 978-1906659-22-6

British Library Cataloguing in Publication Data
A CIP catalogue record for this book can be obtained from the British Library.

Photo of Rodney Hobson by Jamil Shehadeh

Contents

Index of Case Studies

FREE EBOOK VERSION

As a buyer of the print book of *Understanding Company News* you can now download the eBook version free of charge to read on an eBook reader, your smartphone or your computer. Simply go to:

http://ebooks.harriman-house.com/companynews

or point your smartphone at the QRC below.

You can then register and download your free eBook.

FOLLOW US, LIKE US, EMAIL US

@HarrimanHouse
www.linkedin.com/company/harriman-house
www.facebook.com/harrimanhouse
contact@harriman-house.com

 Harriman House

Disclaimer

All the many examples quoted in this book are genuine company announcements issued through the London Stock Exchange. Most have been edited down to pick out the salient points, but in no cases has the wording or the message behind the announcements been changed.

However, they represent the situation at each company at a given moment in time. Circumstances change and issues raised at one juncture may be resolved or superseded. Similarly, new challenges arise over time.

Therefore, nothing in this book constitutes a recommendation to buy or sell shares in any specific company or sector. Investors must exercise their own judgement.

Readers interested in finding out more about a particular company should read the latest stock market announcements. This book explains how to find them and understand them.

About The Author

Rodney Hobson is an experienced financial journalist who has held senior editorial positions with publications in the UK and Asia. Among posts he has held are News Editor for the Business section of *The Times*, Editor of *Shares* magazine, Business Editor of the *Singapore Monitor* and Deputy Business Editor of the *Far Eastern Economic Review*.

He has also contributed to the City pages of the *Daily Mail*, *The Independent* and *The Independent on Sunday*.

Rodney was at the forefront in the setting up of financial websites, firstly as Head of News for the launch of *Citywire* and more recently as Editor of *Hemscott*, for whom he continues to write a weekly investment email. He has appeared on BBC TV and radio and on CNBC, as well as appearing as a guest speaker at conferences such as the World Money Show.

He is the author of *Shares Made Simple*, the authoritative beginner's guide to the stock market, and *Small Companies, Big Profits*, a guide to investing in smaller quoted companies. Both are published by Harriman House.

Rodney is registered as a Representative with the *Financial Services Authority*. He is married with one daughter.

Preface

What the book covers

This book covers announcements issued through the London Stock Exchange by companies with a full stock market listing or whose shares are quoted on the Alternative Investment Market, which is also part of the LSE.

Almost all these announcements, such as annual results, share buying by directors, profit warnings and updates on current trading are required under stock exchange rules or European Union directives. Foreign-based companies that have chosen to have their shares traded in London must abide by the same rules.

While this book is specifically targeted at the UK market, the general principles discussed apply also to overseas stock markets. However, the legal requirements covering what companies must tell shareholders may vary from country to country.

Structure of the book

The book is divided into three sections that help investors to progress easily and logically in understanding what companies tell them.

Section A looks at what the rules are, why they have been imposed and how they have evolved to give private investors a much fairer opportunity to compete with professional investors.

Section B lists and explains the routine statements that all companies issue on a regular basis: trading statements and profit figures. It tells investors what to look for, explains company jargon and shows how to read between the lines when all is not as well as it seems.

Section C considers important announcements, such as profit warnings and directors' share dealings that are issued on an irregular basis as they arise. It explains which announcements are likely to affect the share price and why.

The book is packed full of actual stock market announcements illustrating each point. While these have had to be edited down for reasons of space, the wording is as it appeared and the sense of each announcement has been carefully retained.

Who this book is for

All those baffled shareholders who throw communications from their companies straight into the bin unread desperately need this book. So, too, do investors who read company pronouncements but naively take everything they see at face value.

While this book assumes some basic knowledge of investing and how the stock market works, rank beginners and less sophisticated investors, as well as those who want to widen their knowledge, will benefit from this comprehensive guide to the information that is available, without charge, to private investors on an equal footing with City professionals.

The book is also an invaluable tool for students on business courses and anyone who needs to professionally know about the stock market, such as financial advisers, public relations departments and consultants, company solicitors and stockbrokers. In short, anyone who wants or needs to know about communication between companies and the investment world, including what information companies must release and when, will benefit from reading this book.

In particular, those who have read my beginner's guide to the stock market, *Shares Made Simple*, will progress naturally to this exposition of what companies tell the public.

Supporting websites

The accompanying website for the book can be found at:

www.harriman-house.com/understandingcompanynews

Rodney Hobson's personal website is **www.rodneyhobson.co.uk**.

Introduction

The figures from Arm Holdings looked disappointing: sales down 8%, profits down 2%. Sure enough, the shares were 1% lower within an hour of trading after the results were released.

Yet by the end of the morning Arm shares were *up* more than 1% because investors started to look beyond the figures that had been prominently displayed high in the stock market announcement.

Arm supplies semiconductors with its own programs on them for industries such as mobile phones. The admittedly weak results had been achieved in the teeth of a recession. But, as the company went on to point out, it had in fact gained market share, ameliorating the effect of the downturn by taking business from its rivals.

The wording of company announcements presents different challenges for investors and City professionals. For law firms and financial advisers, the priority is to see that the requirements of UK and European law are complied with alongside London Stock Exchange and Takeover Panel rules; for financial public relations advisers and each company's in-house PR experts, the priority is to put the best gloss on the situation; while for investors the desire is to cut through the jargon and get to the nitty gritty.

It is true that many companies litter their announcements with meaningless phrases such as 'challenging trading conditions' and 'in line with internal company expectations' but they also include all the information needed to invest in the stock market, served up on a plate for those who know where to look and how to interpret the information. This information is published, within fairly narrow limits, at known times, so it is only in unexpected circumstances (such as a takeover bid) that stock market followers should ever be caught out.

By keeping fully informed, all investors can buy and sell shares with confidence, knowing that they have made an informed judgement. By knowing what investors need, company advisers can provide a better service.

Rodney Hobson
October 2009

Section A – The Rules

1.

The Right To Be Informed

The UK's record of preventing insider trading and forcing companies to be frank and upfront with investors has been rightly criticised. In particular, the Serious Fraud Office's record in prosecuting insider traders has been poor and the conviction rate abysmal.

This is in sharp contrast to the situation in the United States, where admittedly the conviction rate is multiplied by plea bargaining and the very expensive legal process, which encourages guilty pleas and accusations against others rather than fighting a lengthy and ruinous case, however worthy the defence.

Nonetheless, the climate for change has come almost imperceptibly in the City. At one time companies would routinely tell newspapers that they were not prepared to comment on rumours. Now it is accepted practice that rumours of major events (such as a takeover approach or a slump in sales) must be confirmed or denied once they are out in the open.

That is only right and proper. Shareholders are entitled to know what is going on in the company that they own. It is quite outrageous if directors – who are after all merely the managers acting on behalf of the owners – feel they have the right to withhold important information.

While the right of the wider investing public to this information is not so clear-cut, it is in the interests of everyone that information should be freely available. The stock exchanges will generate more trades when investors are empowered to make informed decisions, which in turn increases the liquidity that oils the wheels of the market.

Finding a balance

There does admittedly have to be a balance. The board must be able to get on with the day-to-day running of the business and with making longer term strategic plans without having to turn to the shareholders every five minutes for permission to go to the toilet or to blow their noses.

The London Stock Exchange has over several decades made admirable strides towards finding the right balance. Now the internet, where information can be widely circulated in nanoseconds, has transformed the whole investment scene.

The mood has changed towards erring on the side of openness: if in doubt, make an announcement. That attitude will grow as the regulators tighten their grip.

The Wolfson case

Wolfson Microelectronics, a supplier of parts for the electronics industry, was fined £140,000 by the Financial Services Authority in January 2009 for delaying the disclosure of the loss of a major contract for 16 days.

Wolfson was told the previous March that it would not be required to supply parts in future for two iPods made by major customer Apple. Wolfson estimated that this represented a loss of $20 million, or 8% of its forecast revenue for 2008. However, it also expected to make up the shortfall by selling more than it had previously assumed to other customers, so revenue for the year was likely to meet published expectations.

Wolfson discussed the matter with its investor relations advisor, who wrongly recommended that there was no need to disclose the negative news. It was not for another eight days, after directors started to get cold feet at a board meeting, that the company contacted its corporate brokers and lawyers, who recommended disclosing the news.

Even then it took another seven days for an announcement to be made. When the news did emerge, Wolfson shares dropped 18% in one day.

Sceptics will point out that £140,000 is a comparatively small fine for a company of this size. However, the point is that Wolfson did take advice and felt that sales gains elsewhere offset the effect of the loss of the Apple contracts.

The view from the Financial Services Authority was unequivocal. It regarded the loss of sales to Apple as potential inside information and there was an obligation to disclose it. A spokeswoman commented:

> It is unacceptable for a company not to disclose negative news because it believes other matters are likely to offset it. Doing this hampers an investor's ability to make informed decisions and risks distorting the market.

One may feel it was a pity that it took 10 months for the FSA to make this pronouncement, but better late than never. The move towards greater disclosure is inexorable – why take the risk of a fine?

Honesty is the best policy – Barclays

The value of honesty in company announcements was exemplified by Barclays in the depths of the banking crisis. Its shares had slumped along with the rest of the sector, reaching 51.25p compared with 400p only four months earlier.

Although Barclays had apparently avoided ceding control to the government, a fate that befell Royal Bank of Scotland, Lloyds, HBOS and Bradford & Bingley, it was not out of the mire. Despite an injection of £5.3bn from Middle Eastern investors, plus a further £3bn available, it was feared that Barclays would still not have enough capital to survive in the dire circumstances surrounding the international banking sector.

Matters were made worse when RBS warned that its loss for 2008 would be a record £28bn, dwarfing the previous UK highest annual loss of £22bn reported some years earlier by telecoms group Vodafone.

Perhaps stung by press criticism that the board had lost the confidence of investors, the Barclays board resorted to the highly unusual tactic of issuing an open letter from Chairman Marcus Agius and Chief Executive John Varley ahead of the annual results due a couple of weeks later.

It is hard to think of a similar letter ever being issued by a listed company but, as the Barclays pair admitted with some degree of understatement:

Writing in this way ahead of the release of results is unusual, of course, but the turn of events is also unusual.

The key points of the letter were:

Barclays has £36bn of committed equity capital and reserves; we are well funded, and we are profitable. However, we know that our stakeholders want to see the detailed figures for 2008 as quickly as possible. To enable that, we will bring forward the release of our 2008 financial results, as agreed by our auditors, to Monday, 9th February.

We will report a profit before tax for the year well ahead of the consensus estimate of £5.3bn. The profit is struck after all costs, impairment and market valuations. Whilst it includes a number of individually significant items, it mainly reflects strong operating profit generation.

The profit includes the gains arising from the acquisition of the Lehman Brothers North American business, and also the gain on the sale of our closed life business.

Also included in the 2008 results are some £8bn of gross write downs. These figures demonstrate that although we have been heavily impacted by the credit crunch, our income generation was at a record level in 2008 and has enabled us to withstand this impact and still produce strong profits.

As a result of the capital raising announced on 31st October 2008, our capital base has been substantially strengthened in accordance with the capital plan agreed with the UK Financial Services Authority. We calculate that the capital exceeds the regulatory minimum required by the FSA by an amount equivalent to some

£17bn in profit before tax. We confirm that we are not seeking subscription for further capital – either from the private sector or from the UK Government.

Before closing, we should say a word about current trading. Recognising that 2009 is not yet a month old, and that the global economy will remain weak, we can tell you that customer and client activity levels have been high. As a result, we have had a good start to 2009.

This was a kill or cure job. Issuing a highly unusual statement could have spooked the already nervous market; however, if the tactic worked then valuable time had been gained.

Barclays admitted candidly that its Barclays Capital investment arm had run up losses of £8bn, although that would be reduced to £5bn after income and hedging operations were taken into account.

These figures had to be seen in context. They were lower than the equivalent losses admitted by RBS but were higher than Barclays' own first half figures, so further losses had been incurred in the second half.

The vital ingredient of the open letter was a claim that the bank had £17bn in spare capital over and above the regulatory requirement. It would not therefore be necessary to raise more cash, either from the government or from private investors.

Barclays added that it had made a strong start to 2009 with the performance at the previously struggling Barclays Capital particularly strong.

It was worth watching the Barclays share price on the day of the announcement. It jumped 37.5p to 88.7p by the close, a gain of 73%. However, that was lower than the 98p they traded at before RBS spooked the market and much lower than the 153p at which the Qatari investors had agreed to subscribe for shares.

Figure 1.1: Barclays

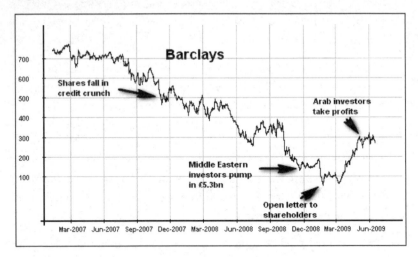

Shareholders needed to consider whether they were sufficiently reassured to stay in for long-term recovery or to take the opportunity presented by the share price rise to cut their losses and get out.

Thanks to the frank attitude of the Barclays board, it proved worth staying in as the shares soon powered to 280p, recovering much more quickly than those of its rivals.

2.
Rules That Companies Must Follow

The European Union tightened its rules in January 2007 with the introduction of its Transparency Directive, so named because it aimed to make quoted companies transparent to shareholders, who would be able to see clearly how well or badly the company was doing. Bad news could not be hidden because investors could, the theory ran, see right through any smokescreens.

The EU, as is its custom, was attempting to harmonise the rules across the continent so that investors could buy shares in companies in any European state confident that the same requirements for openness and fair play were being enforced. This, in the view of the European Commission, would lead to a high level of investor protection throughout the Community.

As is also the way in the EU, it took years to get agreement: the original action plan was published by the European Commission way back in 1999.

To be fair, the outcome was a big improvement on the disparate range of financial reporting requirements previously in existence. The aim was to harmonise the regulations rather than to add to the burden.

Nonetheless, the rules are quite detailed and member states are free to impose additional requirements on companies incorporated in their country. Likewise, individual stock exchanges are able to impose additional requirements on companies whose shares are traded on their markets.

Effect on the UK

Most of the requirements were already pretty much covered on the main market of the London Stock Exchange and, to a lesser extent, on AIM, which is exempt from the directive as it does not, in EU eyes, constitute a proper stock market. Fear not. The LSE imposes strict disclosure requirements on AIM-quoted companies and insists that they appoint an approved nominated adviser to see that they toe the line.

The big change as far as the UK was concerned was to bring in quarterly trading updates rather than the half-yearly pronouncements that typically were issued along with half year and full year results.

The initial proposal was to bring full quarterly reporting, as is the norm in the US. In other words companies would produce accounts every three rather than every six months. There was heavy lobbying against this more onerous requirement on the grounds that it would create an undesirable short term attitude in companies and their shareholders.

Even so, the rules on quarterly statements are still quite detailed, including specifying when they must be published.

The timetable

The Directive says:

> An issuer shall make public a statement by its management during the first six month period of the financial year and another statement by its management during the second six month period.
>
> Such statement shall be made in a period between ten weeks after the beginning and six weeks before the end of the relevant six month period.

You need to look at a calendar to grasp the timetable. For a company whose financial year matches the calendar year, it means that interim statements must be issued somewhere between March 5th and May 14th and between September 4th and November 13th.

For those following the traditional financial year to March 31st, the relevant dates are June 10th to August 19th and between October 9th and December 18th.

Don't worry about the precise dates. The idea is that statements should come out a week or two after the end of the first and third quarters, although the 10-week window is very wide for this purpose.

It means that many companies combine their interim management statement with the issuing of half-yearly or annual results.

When to expect updates

One has to say that companies quoted on the London stock market are playing the game and issuing four reasonably equally spaced trading updates per year. So a company using the calendar year will issue a trading update around March 31st, a second immediately before or after the half year end at June 30th, a third around September 30th and a fourth within days of the full year end at December 31st.

This means you know promptly how the business has performed in each complete quarter.

However, some companies do have leeway to time the updates to suit their particular trading pattern. The most obvious example is in retailing, where companies have traditionally provided an update on how the key Christmas trading period has gone.

There is nothing to stop companies issuing more trading updates than the rules demand. We do occasionally see companies issue updates at the end of each quarter, another update with half year and full year figures and one for good measure at the AGM.

Most companies give advance warning when the next trading statement is due. In some cases each trading update includes a line saying when the next one is due. Sometimes an indication is given within the company results announcements. Other companies issue a separate announcement of an impending update.

In any case you can easily discover when a trading update is likely to be issued by checking the dates on which statements were made in the previous financial year. They tend to be repeated at much the same stage each year.

What the statement contains

The Directive says what should go into the statement:

> It shall contain information that covers the period between the beginning of the relevant six-month period and the date of publication of the statement.
>
> Such a statement shall provide:
>
> - An explanation of *material events and transactions* that have taken place during the relevant period and their impact on the financial position of the issuer and its controlled undertakings, and
>
> - A general description of the *financial position* and *performance* of the issuer and its controlled undertakings during the relevant period.

It is thus no longer possible to hide behind routine 'nothing much has happened' statements that were issued by many companies when quarterly statements started as a fad rather than a legal requirement.

Instead, it is now necessary to provide financial data up to within a few days of the trading update, not only for the main company but for any subsidiaries and joint ventures under its control.

These will not be as detailed as the twice yearly financial results. It would be unreasonable to expect them to be, if they are to be bang up-to-date. Full results take time to compile.

In theory, companies need not produce specific figures. They could include sufficient information in the narrative of the statement. However, that would be difficult to achieve without including key operating statistics such as growth in sales or changes in profit margins.

Recording key events

In addition to any figures, companies are required to record any key events since the previous update and explain the impact. There is wide scope for interpreting what constitutes a material event but the intention is clear: anything that could affect the share price that has not been reported already should be in the quarterly update. Among candidates for inclusion, where relevant, would be:

- changes in the state of the market that the company serves
- large orders received or lost
- refinancing
- acquisitions or disposals
- opening of new premises such as stores, distribution centres or factories
- change in strategy
- progress so far in carrying out a previously announced strategy
- adequacy of finance to fund day-to-day operations or expansion
- new product range
- effects of external events such as foreign exchange rates, energy costs, business rates or wage rates

Bit by bit, quarterly statements have become clearer and more comprehensive so that they now contain much relevant and significant information that the investor ignores at his or her peril.

The downside is that companies are tempted to err on the side of putting an excessive amount of detailed information into the quarterly statements – but that is a price worth paying for being a better informed investor.

Half year results

The Transparency Directive replaced the EU's existing Interim Reporting Directive as regards half yearly and annual results. It requires:

- A report covering the first six months of the financial year as soon as possible after the end of the relevant period, but at the latest within two months

- The report must remain available to the public for at least five years

- It must contain a condensed set of financial statements and an interim management report

The facts and figures given must comply with minimum and quite extensive standards set out in the EU's reporting regulation IAS 34. The main points are:

- Information relating to all material acquisitions, disposals, restructurings and discontinued operations

- If results are split into business or geographic segments, revenue and results for each segment

- Balance sheet comparatives for the last full financial year as well as for the previous first half

- Income statement comparatives for the previous first half

- Cash flow and changes in equity, both with comparatives for the previous first half

- Important events that have occurred during the first six months of the financial year and their impact on the half yearly figures

- Principal risks and uncertainties for the remaining six months of the financial year

If the half-yearly financial report has been audited, which is unusual in the UK, the audit report has to be reproduced in full.

The directors have to give an assurance that the figures and statements give a true and fair view of the company and its financial position.

Annual results

Companies have a little more leeway (four months) to produce their annual financial report, which must also remain publicly available for at least five years. It comprises audited financial statements, accompanied by the auditor's report in full, a management report and an assurance from directors that it is a true and fair record.

The management report must contain (where relevant):

- A fair review of the business and a description of the principal risks and uncertainties that it faces

- A balanced and comprehensive analysis of the development and performance of the business and the position it finds itself in at the end of the year

- Analysis of key financial and other performance indicators including information on matters concerning the environment and employees

- Important events that have occurred since the end of the year

- Likely future development

- Research and development activities

- Information on the acquisition of its own shares

- Details of financial risk management and hedging policies

- Risks involving product prices, credit, liquidity and cash flow

Some items, such as research or hedging, may not be relevant and need not be included.

As with the half yearly statement, directors must guarantee that the financial statement is drawn up to accepted accounting standards and give a true and fair view of the position the business is in.

3.
News Sources

The London Stock Exchange has gone from being a cosy little club meeting in coffee houses to a shares market attracting investors from across the globe, distributing information instantaneously worldwide.

It has taken over 300 years but the momentum has really come in the past 20 years, particularly with the growth of computer technology.

Originally, stock exchange members met to issue a list of stock and commodity prices, at first in the Royal Exchange, where other commodities were traded, and then in coffee houses (because the other traders could not stand the rowdy behaviour of stock brokers). This meant that such information as was available was shared by a small elite. Even they had limited knowledge of how well the companies they were trading in were faring.

The first stock exchange premises were established in 1761, so at least there was a place for information to be distributed, albeit to the favoured few. Formal membership followed in 1801, and in 1822 a rule book established the tentative beginnings of some semblance of fair play.

Subsequently news agencies such as Reuters and Extel distributed stock market news and prices for newspapers to pass on to the general public.

Effectively, however, instant information was the prerogative of City professionals until well after the Second World War. Company results and closing share prices were posted up on the bulletin board at the London Stock Exchange's octangular premises in Old Broad Street.

The modern exchange

It was Big Bang, the deregulation of the stock market in 1986, that began the transformation. Although this was primarily a shake-up of the way that shares were traded, the sweeping away of restrictive practices spelt the beginning of the end for the cosy club trading at an advantage over everyone else.

As trading became electronic, so did the availability of information. At first the stock exchange insisted that all news should be published through the exchange. Computerisation and the dawn of the internet speeded up the spread of information but the exchange at first struggled to process the sheer volume of announcements issued at the start of trading each day.

Companies emailed their announcements to the fledgling financial news websites as well as to the exchange and sometimes results were published on these sites a few minutes before they were issued by the LSE.

The exchange quickly asserted its rights, but the thin end of the wedge was being driven ever deeper. Although the LSE constantly updated its technology, so that all announcements lodged overnight were issued simultaneously at 7am, the exchange eventually volunteered to give up its monopoly on information.

Official news distributors

While the overwhelming majority of announcements still come through the exchange's Regulatory News Service (RNS), other news distributors approved by the Financial Services Authority are allowed to compete provided they make the information widely available to newspapers, news services such as the Press Association and to financial news websites.

These are known as *regulatory information services*. Several have met the FSA's criteria but the two most widely used, apart from the RNS, are:

- PRNewswire (part of United Business Media), and

- Hugin (a European corporate communications specialist).

The initials PRN or HUG on an announcement indicates these two respectively as the source.

Other initials you may see are BZN (Business Wire, part of Warren Buffet's Berkshire Hathaway empire) and CIS (Cision, an international public relations and marketing group).

The FSA has also approved news distribution service Marketwire and German-based information distributor EquityStory.

These alternative services set their own charges and can thus compete with RNS on price if they wish. They are equally efficient and reliable. So far they tend to be used by foreign companies with London listings.

Simultaneously, companies quoted on the stock exchange have come under increased pressure not to leak information to selected newspapers and favoured financial journalists. Remarkably well-informed speculation of impending news had a habit of appearing in the press, particularly the Sunday and Monday papers, to be followed by official confirmation as soon as the stock market reopened.

For the general public, this information is most readily available on financial news websites. It does not matter whether the news is issued through RNS or a rival, it appears on websites at the same moment that it is available to any market trader who subscribes to receive the information direct from the London Stock Exchange onto a trading office computer.

The Internet

The best source of company announcements is the internet, where a variety of websites carry the current day's pronouncements with the most recent at the top, running down the list in chronological order.

In some cases, access to previous statements over several years is possible although you may have to pay for the privilege of seeing past announcements.

If you do not have internet access then, frankly, you are at a severe disadvantage in buying and selling shares. There is no other ready source of instant information for the private investor.

Shareholders are entitled to annual and half-yearly results from the company, plus details of any issues that they are required to vote on, such as a rights issue or a takeover, but paper-based information comes by second class post.

The great thing about the internet is that you can see announcements in full and at the same moment that City traders gain access to them. It is also possible to set up filters so that announcements from companies you specify ping up on your computer.

Websites for investors

InvestEgate

Possibly the best site, in terms of the amount of information available and easy access to it, is InvestEgate (website **www.investegate.co.uk**). Log on and you go straight to the current day's announcements. A search facility on the same page allows you to call up past announcements and the archive goes back further than most alternative sites. You can see announcements for any day since 1 January 2002.

Hemscott

Hemscott (**www.hemscott.com**) has the current day's announcements in full. You will have to register but the service is free on its company news section. However, you need to subscribe to its Premium service to gain access to past announcements.

One mixed blessing on Hemscott is that the list of announcements is liberally interspersed with Dow Jones reports, foreign exchange data and much else, including sport headlines! You get some comment and interpretation of the announcements, with the key points picked out for you.

This is not a complete substitute for you reading the announcements yourself and making your own judgements but it does help the less experienced investor to understand what companies are saying and to highlight those companies that may be of interest.

The Dow Jones reports provide useful interpretation of the day's announcements but there will be several write-ups on each announcement so it can be quite a trawl to get what you want.

ADVFN

You also need to register with ADVFN (**www.advfn.com**) for access to its free service. The news section contains a brief summary of what each announcement is, which makes the page somewhat lengthy. A big plus is that companies whose share price has moved furthest on the back of the announcement are featured prominently at the top of the page and the other announcements are grouped into sectors so you can check any sector you are particularly interested in.

Past announcements for each quoted company are available free through the search facility but you need to know the stock exchange code for each stock.

MoneyAM

MoneyAM (**www.moneyam.com**) has about a dozen of the day's announcements on its news page. For all the past month's announcements, click on All Articles. It is possible to go further back chronologically or call up announcements from individual companies or specific types of announcements on the search facility. This service is free.

Digital Look

Digital Look (**www.digitallook.com**) has a company announcements page and a facility to call up previous announcements from individual companies.

Other sites

The London Stock Exchange website (**www.londonstockexchange.com**) is not particularly useful for finding the current day's announcements as only a limited number of the most recent ones are shown.

The most useful research facility on the LSE site is the comprehensive company reports giving a five-year overview of each quoted company's strengths, weaknesses and financial trends.

If you use an online broker it may be useful to use its news pages. For instance, Selftrade (**selftrade.co.uk**) carries RNS announcements within its Market News section.

> Remember that websites evolve over time so what is available, and what charges are made, are subject to change.

Section B – Regular Statements

4.
Trading Statements

By far the most important announcements issued on a regular basis are the trading statements. We have noted that interim management statements must be issued roughly one quarter and three quarters of the way through the financial year. Other updates tend to be forthcoming at half year and year end and at annual general meetings.

An update on current trading will also usually be included in any results announcement. If a company becomes involved on either side of a takeover bid, or makes a rights issue or placing, it is likely to give guidance on current trading as part of the rationale for the action it is taking.

Trading statements tell you what is happening here and now. They tell you if sales and profitability have changed in recent weeks, for better or worse; if the markets the company operates in are improving or deteriorating; which parts of the business are soaring and which are struggling; and how management sees the immediate future panning out.

They tend to be less detailed than the actual results announcements and, in particular, do not normally include profits figures or proposed dividends. However, they are a better guide to the future than results, which cover a period that is in the past.

A basic statement

Trading statements range from the bland to the highly detailed. They may be quite short and straightforward, as is this one from Spring, which specialises in recruiting professional staff:

> In common with our peers, the current economic environment has proven to be challenging in the first quarter. Notwithstanding this we have produced results in line with our expectations to date.
>
> Our Contract business, which accounts for approximately 80% of our Net Fee Income, experienced a 3% reduction, performing creditably against the market. In our Permanent divisions which have historically accounted for around 20% of net fee income we experienced a 42% fall which has tracked in line with the sector. This has resulted in a total reduction of 12% in net fee income year on year.
>
> The new offices opened in 2008 in Italy, France and Asia Pacific, whilst still in investment phase, are all performing in line with our expectations. We believe that this ongoing investment will put us in a strong position to support our future growth.

What this tells you

Although this statement is fairly short, it is packed with vital information that allows investors to assess the immediate prospects for the company.

As more pedantic readers will note from the first sentence, grammar is not always a strong point in company announcements and companies do like using fashionable words such as "challenging", which can be quite ambiguous.

Challenging? We need to consider whether we think management is up to the challenge. Always view such terms with a critical eye.

However, it is clear that the whole sector has seen a downturn in activity. Spring is performing in line with management expectations, which implies that there has been little change since the previous update.

There is also an implication that the company's fortunes are pretty well tied to those of the sector. Any recovery (or further deterioration) is likely to depend on how the recruitment market as a whole performs rather than on any action taken by Spring.

We do have some figures that allow us to be more specific. Supplying staff on short term contracts, which is by far the larger part of the business, is down only 3% while the biggest hit has been taken by the much smaller permanent placings side. That is mildly reassuring, except that income is still down 12% overall.

This statement was issued in the teeth of recession so one may feel that a 12% fall was not too bad in the circumstances.

Spring has been expanding abroad, a sensible move that means a downturn in the UK could be offset by better times elsewhere. Unfortunately these are still early days and the prognosis from Europe and Asia is quite downbeat. You can rest assured that if there was anything to gloat about Spring would certainly have been banging on about how well its overseas expansion was doing in order to deflect shareholders' attention from troubles at home.

How the shares moved

Trading statements need to be read in conjunction with changes in the share price to see how the market views the company's prospects. Investors hope to spot an opportunity that the market has missed; alternatively they may feel that any news is fully reflected in the share price.

Spring shares had already fallen from 80p in the middle of 2007 to a low of 20p at the end of 2008, reflecting concerns that professional staff were being fired rather than recruited.

Figure 4.1: Spring

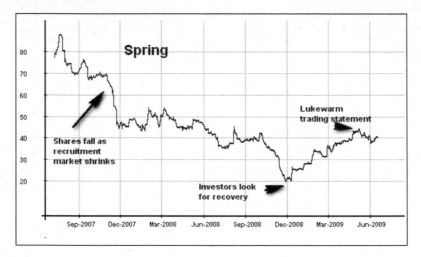

As so often happens on the stock market, the fall was overdone and Spring shares had been recovering for the five months running up to the trading statement, reaching 41p. The best buying opportunity had thus been missed but the shares were maintaining an upward momentum.

Investors needed to ask themselves whether this rather downbeat statement justified a doubling of the share price over the previous five months or whether prospects were any better than they were a couple of years earlier when the share price was double its current level.

Detailed statements

In contrast to the short, matter-of-fact update from Spring, trading statement can be quite detailed, especially if a company has expanded into a global operation, as is the case with building materials supplier Wolseley:

Pre Close Period Trading Statement for the five months ended 31 December 2008

Overview

- Further deterioration in Wolseley's general trading environment in November and December due to unprecedented events in the global financial markets and negative GDP trends.

- Management's emphasis continues to be concentrated on actions to enhance cash generation and reduce costs, with benefits coming through as planned.

- Recent adverse movement in foreign exchange rates have negatively affected the Group's overall net debt position. However, the Group's projections continue to show covenant compliance at 31 January 2009.

Operating Highlights

- Revenue up c.3%, down c.10% in constant currency.

- Trading profit down c.45%, c.52% in constant currency.

- Profit before tax, exceptional items and amortisation and impairment of acquired intangibles down c.66%, c.75% in constant currency.

- Net debt increased by 22% since 31 July 2008 to £3 billion principally due to £557 million adverse effect of currency exchange. However, net debt is expected to be lower at 31 January 2009 due to an expected working capital inflow, but will be dependent on exchange rates at that date.

Debt Reduction and Restructuring Actions

- Previously announced actions to date initiated in the five months to 31 December 2008 have resulted in headcount reductions of 7,500, combined exceptional restructuring charges of £208 million, and annualised cost savings of £237 million.

- Recent actions in the period to 31 December 2008 have resulted in additional exceptional restructuring charges of around £39 million and annualised savings of around £93 million.

Outlook

- The Group expects macro economic conditions to deteriorate in the short term, and until conditions stabilise Wolseley is unlikely to see any upturn in its markets.

- Until consumer confidence returns and availability of finance for customer projects improves, the Group expects performance in North America to decline.

- The Group also expects conditions in the UK to continue to deteriorate with performance in Continental Europe also likely to remain under pressure as consumer sentiment is further negatively affected by macro economic conditions.

These points were all expanded in a lengthy statement which, to its credit, went into some detail about trading conditions in the areas where Wolseley operates.

Wolseley had once been one of the great stock market success stories. Having expanded strongly but sensibly in the UK, it set out to make a similar job of it in the US. Transatlantic transplants are notoriously hard to pull off but Wolseley seemed to have done it as the housing market continued to grow, if a little erratically, on both sides of the pond. The group also made inroads into Continental Europe.

Being in the US and Europe gave Wolseley an alternative market to rely on during any downturn in the UK. Furthermore, the group sensibly diversified away from its traditional plumbing products business into other construction related areas such as timber supplies, including products for commercial property.

The only thing that could possibly go wrong was a collapse in the housing market on both sides of the Atlantic. And that, unfortunately, was what happened.

The story so far

Wolseley's statement issued in January 2009 followed a series of poor results, profit warnings and the laying off of staff. It was worth going back over previous announcements to put the latest news into the context of a long downturn, with events outside Wolseley's control.

Critics could reasonably claim that Wolseley had been slow to react to the initial setbacks in the US housing market, where the sub-prime scandal began. Previous trading statements indicated that cutbacks in the US and a reduction in the business there had been made too slowly to save the group from a nasty knock.

Thus Wolseley had been forced into more and more drastic efforts to survive the crisis.

The current situation

The latest statement showed underlying pre-tax profits down 75%. That excluded exceptional costs, writing off the value of assets and the effects of currency changes.

Meanwhile debt had increased by 22% to £3bn over the space of only five months, partly because most borrowings were in dollars and euros which had appreciated against the weak pound – 14% of net debt was denominated in US dollars, 48% in euros and 38% in sterling.

It is always important to note the effects of currency changes on companies with overseas operations. The sensible ones try to align debt with income, so if half of income in is dollars then half of borrowings should be in dollars also. Wolseley had admittedly endeavoured to follow this maxim but was caught out by the sharpness of the decline in the US building industry.

Investors did well to read the section labelled Outlook with a sceptical eye. A further economic deterioration would surely make matters worse, so the ominous phrase 'unlikely to see any upturn in its markets' was, if anything, over optimistic.

Any further downturn in markets would surely lead to a further deterioration in Wolseley's results. Standing still would actually be an achievement.

Indeed, chief executive Chip Hornsby admitted as much in the following day's newspapers where he was quoted as saying:

It is hard to predict when we will reach the bottom.

That phrase was not in the trading statement but the implication was there for those with a critical eye.

Managing debt

This caveat did admittedly need to be read in conjunction with the claim that Wolseley was not in imminent danger of breaching its banking covenants (the terms laid down by its lenders). Closer inspection of this claim showed that it effectively lasted only to the end of the month:

> Due principally to the unprecedented movement in currency exchange rates in the last three months, the Group's covenant headroom at 31 January 2009 is likely to be lower than we expected at the time of our interim management statement. The final net debt position at that date should be lower than at 31 December 2008 due to an expected working capital inflow, although it will be dependent on foreign exchange rates at 31 January 2009. The Group's projections continue to show compliance with our banking covenants at 31 January 2009.

This would inevitably lead to speculation that Wolseley would soon be forced to go cap in hand to the banks, a move that tends to lead to more onerous interest rates being imposed. Asking for new borrowing terms at a time when banks were themselves struggling to rebuild their profits and balance sheets would be singularly uncomfortable.

A further sign that Wolseley was far from being out of the woods was news that another 7,500 jobs had been shed over the previous five months, taking total job losses to 15,000. In other words, half the job losses had come more than a year after the scale of the US sub-prime disaster was widely known. And more job cuts were still being considered.

The latest round of job losses was set to save £237m a year. The trouble with sacking people, apart from the human misery for those losing their jobs, is that redundancy money has to be paid up front while the savings from wages take time to start flowing through. Indeed, it can often be the case that the last jobs are going just when a company needs to be thinking about recruiting for recovery.

Raising cash

Right at the end of the statement, Wolseley indicated that it was looking to raise cash through the sale of assets and possible by issuing more shares, though this final paragraph did not spell that out clearly:

> The Group will continue to evaluate all of the options and implement the actions necessary to position the balance sheet appropriately for the medium term. The next few months will be critical in providing further evidence to assess how the downturn may evolve. The Group's objective is to position itself to be able to continue to operate competitively, and maintain a level of investment over the medium term that will ensure the business is well positioned to benefit when the economies in which it operates stabilise and markets begin to recover.

Paragraphs like this one seem superficially to say a lot, but when you look at them more closely they really tell you very little. Surely you would expect any company to continue to evaluate all its options.

Similarly the remark that it would 'position the balance sheet appropriately'. This means that Wolseley was reassessing how much debt it ought to carry for the foreseeable future. Again, you would expect this to be the norm.

This phrase was especially curious because, in the expanded section on debt, we found the following sentence:

> The Group has committed and undrawn banking facilities available of over £1 billion as at 31 December 2008 and has no need for additional facilities until after the year ended 31 July 2011.

This means that the banks have agreed to lend Wolseley more than £1 billion but none of this money has been used yet. Shareholders were entitled to wonder why the balance sheet needed to be 'repositioned' if such a large sum of money was ready and waiting at the bank.

Selling assets versus issuing shares

When a company puts remarks about considering options and repositioning debt in its statement that means it sees the need to take drastic action soon, hence the assumption that parts of the business might be sold off and cash raised through issuing more shares. These are the two quick routes to reducing debt to more manageable proportions.

In such circumstances there is a real danger that assets would be sold at distressed prices, given that everyone in the building sector was suffering from the same problems as Wolseley.

Issuing more shares in a placing would dilute the holdings of existing shareholders and, given the 28% fall in the shares over the previous 12 months, the issue price would have to be at a deep discount to the existing stock market price.

Existing shareholders might be left with an uncomfortable choice if Wolseley decided to go for a rights issue rather than a placing.

Wolseley shares fell 30% to 1201p on the day of this discouraging announcement.

Figure 4.2: Wolseley

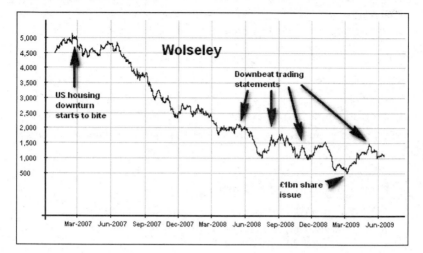

Investors needed to consider at what point they might start to recover. Chief Executive Chip Hornsby claimed that Wolseley was taking market share from regional construction suppliers in the US that had gone bust in the downturn. He argued that the US would be the first market to recover because it was at least one quarter ahead of the UK in terms of job losses and economic slowdown.

The arguments were hardly persuasive and it looked premature to pile in at that stage. Nonetheless, it was worth keeping tabs on Wolseley as it stood to gain when the economies in which it operated started to recover.

Seen in context

We referred, when studying the Wolseley statement, to the importance of reading trading statements in the context of the company and its trading environment. This was well demonstrated by a routine update from newspaper and stationery retailer WHSmith covering the 20 weeks to 17 January.

It is customary for retailers to put out trading updates in January to give investors an idea of how the key Christmas period has gone. Many retailers make most of their profits in November to January – indeed, before its demise, the retailing arm of Woolworths made all its profits in the final three months of the year and ran at a loss for the other nine.

In the case of WHSmith, newspapers and magazines are a year-round phenomenon, which is good news because it leaves Smith less vulnerable to seasonal variations. The stationery side is keyed into the back-to-school bonanza in August while books, CDs and DVDs are more geared to Christmas present buying. Here is the main part of a trading statement issued by WHSmith:

Profits in line with expectations

WHSmith is today providing an update on its trading performance for the 9 weeks and the 20 weeks to 17 January 2009.

Group total sales were flat with like for like (LFL) sales down 5% for the 20 weeks.

The Group delivered a solid performance. In our High Street division we continued to deliver our strategy in a challenging trading period. In our Travel division we made progress in a tough environment. We increased gross margins and maintained tight cost control across both divisions.

In High Street, LFL sales for the 9 and 20 weeks were down 7% and 7% respectively and gross margin improved strongly year on year, reflecting the performance of Entertainment. Excluding Entertainment, LFL sales for the 9 and 20 weeks were down 3%.

In Travel, total sales were up 20% and LFL sales were down 1% for the 20 weeks. Sales continued to outperform passenger numbers and gross margin improved further.

The headline on the announcement was not particularly inspiring, saying the profits were in line with expectations. While there was no nasty shock, nor was there a pleasant surprise. Also, there is no mention of sales in the headline, so one should immediately suspect bad news on that front, particularly as other retailers had been whining on about what a poor festive season it had been.

Sales and margins

To be fair, Smith did put high in the text that total sales were flat and like-for-like sales were down on the same period for the previous year.

It is important to distinguish between total and like-for-like sales (often abbreviated to LFL), as the latter gives a fairer comparison, particularly with retailers. If a retail chain opens more stores you would expect total sales to rise. Similarly, an increase in floor space at an existing store ought to increase sales. Further distortions can come from revamping or refurbishing stores.

On the other hand, sales may fall if stores are closed. Where a chain closes poorly performing outlets, a fall in total sales is a price worth paying, especially if the outlets in question are loss makers.

The like-for-like sales figure cuts out the distortions by comparing only those outlets that have traded through the latest period and also traded throughout the comparable period a year earlier.

The third paragraph says very little except that it does make the important point that gross margins were increased. Margins are profit margins, the percentage extra that the business is able to add to its selling price on top of its overall costs. The higher the margins, the more profitable sales are.

This is an important line in any trading statement, especially in tough trading conditions. Businesses have to make a calculated decision whether to try to maintain sales by cutting prices, and therefore profit margins, or whether to sacrifice sales by maintaining prices and profit margins.

This decision is particularly important in the highly competitive world of retailing, where price promotions are a way of life.

The other part of this equation is costs. If selling prices can be maintained while costs are reduced, then profit margins can be increased. Again, this is particularly important in retailing, though it applies to some extent to all businesses.

Many costs for retailers are fixed or even rising out of the control of the business. Minimum wages, set by Government and increasing each year, are widespread in the sector; business rates also go up rather than down; shops must be lit and heated at prices set by power suppliers; distribution and warehousing is often carried out by third parties.

So, news that gross margins had improved is welcome, although the statement does not give specific figures so it is hard to assess just how good the news is. Likewise it is good to hear that costs have been tightly controlled but at the end of the day what does this actually mean? Again, Smith offers no specifics.

Beware of accepting bland generalisations. Companies tend to put the best slant on the situation that they can.

For better or worse

We do get specifics on High Street sales, which are down 7% over the past seven weeks, the same figure as for the past 20 weeks. This is useful as we can see whether the situation is getting worse or better. In this case sales have neither deteriorated or improved.

It is always worth checking back on what was happening a year ago. Did the company have a particularly strong trading period 12 months earlier, in which case weak figures are more excusable as they are up against tough comparable figures? Did the company struggle a year ago, in which case we would expect to see some recovery this time and weak figures would indicate a continuing downward spiral?

We have a sales figure for the past 20 weeks. What happened before that? Were sales better or worse six months ago? Some companies, notably Marks & Spencer and some supermarkets, often give the past four quarterly figures so we can easily detect the trend. Otherwise, you must look back at the figures yourself. Identifying a trend is well worth the effort even if it is a little painstaking.

That's Entertainment

Another point on which this statement is less than helpful is the enigmatic reference to Entertainment, which has clearly dragged down the High Street figures by four percentage points.

This refers, in fact, to the failure of Woolworth's Entertainment UK distribution arm, which provided some CD and DVD products to Smith and which collapsed into administration during the key Christmas period. The WHSmith trading statement, rather unhelpfully, gives no indication of whether this disruption to supplies is continuing or whether other sources have been found.

The travel division refers to outlets at railway stations and airports. This side of the business has done better than the High Street shops so it is disappointing to see that, although total sales are higher, there is a slight dip in like-for-like sales. Again, Smith declines to say whether the situation has got better or worse.

Sales increases must have come from opening new outlets, which costs money in terms of the one-off expense of setting up each outlet plus continuing running costs from staff, electricity and distribution. Smith points out that sales from these outlets are growing faster than passenger numbers. So they should. If there are more outlets, then passengers have more opportunity to buy from Smith rather than go to an alternative retailer or do without a book to read on the journey.

The chief executive's comments

The first paragraph of comment from chief executive Kate Swann is generalised and, when you analyse it closely, tells us little if anything.

> Commenting on today's announcement, Kate Swann, Group Chief Executive said:
>
> "As anticipated, trading conditions on the high street were challenging over the Christmas period. However, we continue to successfully deliver our strategy and maintain operational

> flexibility, increasing gross margins and accelerating our cost reduction plans. We are pleased with the progress in our Travel business, despite the expected weaker passenger numbers in Air."

Chief executives are as prone as the rest of us to use words and phrases that are in vogue. Thus the word 'challenging' appears. It has the great charm (from a chief executive's point of view) of covering a multitude of sins while setting out an excuse if trading turns nasty. It carries implications of 'well, I did warn you' and 'it wasn't my fault' for future use.

And what on earth does 'operational flexibility' mean?

However, we can understand that Swann's preference is to increase profit margins rather than resort to slashing prices, even if that means losing some sales. This goes some way to explaining why sales have stagnated over recent weeks. It would have been useful to see specific figures for the claimed improvement in margins so we could have a better assessment of how well the strategy is working.

The second paragraph of Swann's comments makes clear that trading conditions are likely to continue to be difficult:

> Looking ahead, we expect consumer spending in our markets to remain subdued and we have planned accordingly.

In all, this is not a particularly encouraging statement. Total sales are flat, sales per store are down and trading is tough.

The overall picture

However, investors should see this statement in the light of the performance of WHSmith over the past few years, in particular during the time that Kate Swann has been at the helm.

Like many long-established businesses, WHSmith had been slow to adapt to the modern world, lurching from one unsuccessful initiative to another. When Swann took over as chief executive in November 2003 there was a widespread expectation of failure.

It is very difficult for women to get to the top in any major company. Often they get the job that men will not touch for fear it is tainted with failure. The corollary is that women try harder, knowing that they rarely get a second chance at a big prize.

In the event, Swann proved to be well up to the job and she engineered a slow but tangible improvement in Smith's fortunes. In particular, she cut back on the struggling High Street chain and expanded in the travel outlets at airports and railway stations where there was a captive audience.

The references to trading in the Travel section, where Smith is doing clearly better than in the High Street, should be read in this context. Total sales are up 20% and like-for-likes have dipped just 1%, much less than in the High Street, despite the resistance to chasing sales at any price.

We should note that Travel sales have risen faster than passenger numbers and that profit margins have improved.

So the overall picture is that WHSmith shares should be treated with caution but certainly not spurned.

Sales figures

Trading statements are particularly important in the case of retailers, where sales figures can vary from season to season.

Here are sales figures from retailer Marks & Spencer covering the final quarter of its financial year to the end of March 2009, a time when retailers were under heavy pressure from rising costs and falling consumer spending on the High Street.

In common with other retailers, M&S gives figures for 13 weeks rather than for three calendar months. This avoids any distortion caused by the fact that some days produce higher sales than others: including an extra Saturday or late night shopping day this year compared with last would artificially inflate the figures.

Note the downside of this: the year end date will creep earlier each year (52 weeks is 364 days, one short of the 365 calendar year) until an extra week has to be added to bring the year end back to the end of March.

Here are the highlights:

13 weeks to 28 March 2009

- Group sales up 1.9%

- UK sales down 0.3%: General Merchandise -1.2% (Clothing -1.0%; Home -2.3%); Food +0.4%

- UK like for like sales down 4.2%: General Merchandise -4.8%; Food -3.7%

- Online Sales up 20%

- International sales up 23%

Adjusting for the timing of Easter (March 2008 vs April 2009) would add c.0.7% to both General Merchandise and Food sales.

While M&S sales were higher overall, this was because of expansion overseas, where sales increased 23%. While this increase looks impressive, it should be remembered that the overseas side is comparatively small, hence the comparatively small increase in total group sales.

The UK tells a different story, with sales down overall and also on a like-for-like basis.

Assessing different parts of the business

Marks & Spencer always clearly divides its figures into understandable categories so we can see instantly how the different parts of the business are faring.

It is immediately clear that home sales are suffering most. There is some comfort in the fact that this is the section for which M&S is least known for. The chain could, at a pinch, scale back on this section – it is not available in all stores anyway – and concentrate more on clothing and food.

More worrying is the poor performance of clothing, which when added to home makes up general merchandising. Clothing is under pressure from cut-price competitors and has not responded sufficiently from advertising.

Food, which has also been heavily advertised, has at least shown increased sales overall, although like-for-like sales are lower.

There is some encouragement in the big increase in online sales. Retailers with a strong online presence have a better chance of surviving in the cut-throat environment. Some of the largest chains have been slowest to harness the selling power of the internet so there is hope for more improvement.

Always read the small print. M&S has actually done better than the bare figures suggest. The previous year Easter, a heavy selling period because more people have time to wander round the shops, fell early and came within the final quarter. This time it is later and the impact is missing.

Allowing for Easter, general merchandising sales would have been down only 0.5% and food would have been up 1.1%, giving an overall gain.

Comparing with the previous quarter

It is also important to get sales figures in perspective. The previous batch covering the 13 weeks to 27 December showed:

- Group sales down 1.2%

- UK sales down 3.4%: General Merchandise -5.5% (Clothing -6.5%; Home +1.0%) ; Food -1.1%

- UK like-for-like sales down 7.1%: General Merchandise -8.9%; Food -5.2%

- Online sales up 29%

- International sales up 26.9%

So there has on the whole been a considerable improvement compared with these earlier figures. Total sales are now up on the previous year instead of down; the slide in UK sales has been virtually eliminated; clothing is much improved; food is recovering from an alarming slide. Only home sales in the UK, the smallest part, have swung the wrong way.

However, those online and overseas sales improvements in the latest quarter don't look quite as rosy. These sales are not growing as quickly as they did in the previous quarter.

Comparing business segments

Chairman Sir Stuart Rose puts into perspective the two main business segments in the latest review. First food:

> Food's performance improved again, with customers welcoming our increased innovation, better ranging and sharper values highlighted by our Wise Buys, Dine In and Family Favourite offers. We continue to improve availability.

Retailers like phrases with the word 'value' in them, though one hopes that they are always trying to provide value across the range. Sharper values presumably implies unusually good value – high quality at a lower price – but it is always best to be sceptical of such ambiguous turns of phrase.

Availability is, however, indisputably important. If the goods are not readily available on the shelves they will not sell – however much value is offered. Retailers tread a narrow line between overstocking with goods that do not sell and therefore have to be sold off cheaply at the end of the season and understocking so that items vanish from the shelves and the opportunity to sell more is lost.

Then clothing:

> We maintained market share in Clothing over the full year.

So clothing is likely to be a continuing problem. The whole market is down just as much as M&S. If this trend continues, M&S will need to gain market share just to stand still.

Two for the price of one

Just because you have seen a trading statement from a company you are interested in, you should not assume that you can close your eyes and ears for another three months. Further updates may be forthcoming.

Retailers in particular are prolific in issuing trading updates; and shareholders in specialist retailer JD Sports got two statements within a month of each other. The first covered the Christmas trading period, including the early January sales. Because this period is so important to most retailers, it is normal for each chain to put out an update early in January.

Shareholders are thus informed of whether Santa called this year and also whether any leftover stock was cleared during the days following Christmas, when goods are traditionally sold off at reduced prices.

The update from JD was eagerly awaited. The company had gone through difficult times, as had other sports goods retailers. Sales tend to be boosted by major sporting events and there were long gaps to the next Ashes series, the soccer World Cup, the Rugby World Cup and the London Olympics.

While JD was able to report 'a positive sales performance' over the festive season, its directors decided to put in a dampener so that investors did not get too carried away with enthusiasm. They pointed out, quite reasonably in the prevailing economic climate, that sales might well slip back in the early part of the new year.

Like most retailers, JD has set its financial year to run to the end of January when there is some respite after the busiest period of the year but it is well before Easter, which, being a moveable feast, tends to distort trading patterns.

JD thus issued another trading update just after its financial year drew to a close. This indicated that the better performance had in fact continued.

> Following the trading update on 9 January 2009, where we reported a positive sales performance for the Christmas period, management prudently anticipated that given the current general retail

> environment negative sales would prevail in the early part of the calendar year 2009.
>
> The Board are pleased to report that the positive sales uplift reported for the Christmas trading period has in fact been sustained during January. As a consequence Management confidently expects that the Group's profit before tax and exceptional items for the year ended 31 January 2009 will marginally exceed current market expectations.

Investors should be aware that companies are increasingly taking a more cautious line. This eliminates awkward questions that arise when companies have been unduly optimistic and get caught out. But an added factor is that a cautious note tacked onto an upbeat report does no harm and it looks good to trumpet a better than expected performance later.

Sector comparisons

It is always worthwhile comparing announcements from companies in the same sector. Are they all singing from the same hymn sheet?

If one company is doing well, it could be because the whole sector is buoyant, in which case it is worth checking whether shares in rival companies are worth buying before they too reveal good news.

On the other hand, one successful company could be taking sales from less efficient competitors and this could be a signal to get out if you hold shares in a rival.

Fortunately trading statements give clues as to which is the case. Look out particularly for references to 'market share'. If someone is gaining a greater share of the market, then someone else is losing it.

Look also for indications of whether the market as a whole is growing. Where a company claims to be gaining a larger share of a shrinking market, this may indicate that its own sales are falling – it's just that everyone else is doing even worse.

Even where a whole sector is growing there will be bigger winners and smaller winners. For instance, when Tesco was growing rapidly the rest of the supermarket sector was also growing – but not as rapidly and there were some losers: Sainsbury's had a spell in the doldrums; Morrisons struggled for a time after taking over Safeway, which had itself lost ground badly while supermarkets generally were taking trade away from corner shops.

Look at what is happening to profit margins: if these are being squeezed, then sales are being won at the expense of profits.

Comparing supermarkets

The three main UK supermarket chains (excluding Asda, as its shares are not quoted) reported on Christmas trading, giving an opportunity to make comparisons. In the order that the updates were released, here are the main points for comparison:

Sainsbury's

Third Quarter Trading Statement for 13 weeks to 3 January 2009

- Total sales for third quarter up 4.8% (5.3% excluding fuel)

- Like-for-like sales for third quarter up 3.9% (4.5% excluding fuel)

Tesco

Group sales increased by 11.6% during the seven weeks to 10 January 2009, driven by continued rapid international expansion and steady growth in the UK. In the UK, like-for-like sales excluding petrol increased by 2.5% in the period.

Morrisons

In the 6 weeks to 4 January 2009 total sales excluding fuel were up by 9.4% (7.7% including fuel), of which 1.2% was a contribution from new space. Like for like sales excluding fuel increased by 8.2% (6.6% including fuel).

We do need to exercise a little caution in interpreting these figures because:

• Rather annoyingly, supermarkets tend not to report on exactly the same periods. While the period ends are in this case only a week apart, the periods covered vary from six to 13 weeks.

• We need to distinguish between fuel and non-fuel sales. Figures excluding fuel are more reliable because the fluctuating price of fuel causes distortions.

• Total sales include new store openings. Like-for-like sales figures give a more accurate picture of changes year on year.

• Tesco has been expanding abroad and its total sales figures are heavily boosted by overseas operations that are growing rapidly.

Nonetheless the fortunes of the three rivals at this particular juncture are sufficiently distinct: Morrisons is continuing its recovery with like-for-like sales growth, excluding fuel, of 8.2%. The comparable figure from Sainsbury's is 4.5% and for Tesco 2.5%.

Hide and seek

It really does pay to look carefully through trading statements. Often the most important news is in one paragraph buried away among a mass of information.

A trading statement issued by building products supplier SIG included the following as the 18th out of 20 paragraphs.

> In order to better align resources to anticipated levels of trading going into 2009, SIG has taken some additional cost saving measures to those previously announced in its November 2008 IMS. The total number of branch closures has increased to 80, with a headcount reduction including head office functions of c.1,000 or 7.5% of total staffing. From these actions we expect to deliver an anticipated incremental cost saving in total in 2009 of over £27m. The associated one-off restructuring costs of c.£22m will be treated as non-recurring items in the 2008 accounts.

I am not suggesting that SIG tried to hide this information. The trading statement did in fact clearly set out the current trading situation in its various markets. However, this was the paragraph that most affected the share price that day and you had to read down to find it.

It is a bit of a mealy mouthed start, but then you have to get used to that in reading company statements. What the first few words mean in plain English is that SIG is cutting back on jobs and branches because it expects sales to fall.

This is bad news, since SIG had already embarked on cutbacks only a couple of months earlier so the implication is that trading is worse than previously expected. You have to compare this statement with the previous one to find the extent of the deterioration, as SIG does not want to spell it out.

Research will show you that the number of proposed branch closures has increased from 65 to 80 and job losses from 900 to 1,000 – not a drastic increase, so it is surprising that SIG did not make this clear.

It does mean, though, sacking 7.5% of its workforce according to the statement.

This headcount reduction will save over £27m a year – companies like to use the word incremental in this context to mean annual – but it will cost about £22m.

That SIG is treating this as a one-off expense in its accounts is neither here nor there. The amount is the same whatever you call it. Nor does the treatment of the figures alter the fact that the costs will be incurred first and the savings will come later.

Figure 4.3: SIG

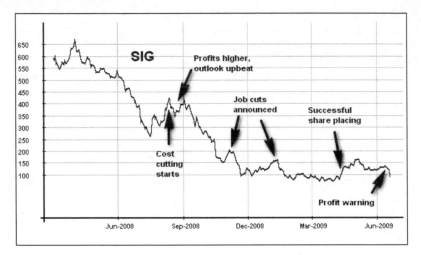

SIG shares fell 17% on the day of this announcement. That fall was caused by paragraph 18. Those who got out were entitled to feel a little smug only weeks later when SIG told the stock exchange:

> The Board confirms that it is considering a range of options including a potential equity raising. A further announcement will be made as and when appropriate.

This announcement was forced by a newspaper report in the *Sunday Telegraph* that SIG, Europe's largest supplier of insulation, had asked its brokers to sound out major shareholders about a possible rights issue – rivals such as Wolseley and CRH had already raised more than £2 billion between them after a serious decline in the building materials sector.

The choices available

Because the newspaper report specifically mentioned issuing shares, SIG was obliged to admit that equity raising (the issuing of more shares) was one option. Otherwise it was in no mood to go into details, possibly because it was still early days and nothing had yet been decided.

Had plans been advanced, it would have been easier to be more specific, although the AGM was looming and it was possible that SIG wanted to unveil its plans on the big day.

Options open to SIG were:

- Borrow more from the banks. This option was limited given the reluctance of banks to lend during the credit crunch.

- Issue corporate bonds. Likewise difficult in the circumstances.

- Sell parts of the business. This would probably raise too little money and involve selling businesses at heavily reduced prices given that others in the business who might want to buy were short of cash themselves.

- Place shares with major institutions, provided enough institutions were prepared to put up cash at around the current share price.

- Make a placing and open offer under which institutions would buy shares but existing small shareholders would have the opportunity to take part.

- Make a rights issue in which all existing shareholders subscribe for new shares according to a ratio fixed by the company.

Given the financial and economic circumstances, SIG might find most of these options impossible or unattractive. The trouble was that SIG needed to raise enough cash to make a significant dent in its debts at a time when its share price had fallen heavily over several months.

5.

Profit Figures

Companies whose shares are traded on either the main board of the London Stock Exchange or on AIM must produce profits figures at least twice a year, one set of figures covering the first half of their financial year and the second set covering the whole year (which may comprise 12 calendar months or 52 weeks).

There are two circumstances in which a set of figures may be produced for a shorter period.

The more common one is that the company produces quarterly figures. This tends to happen with companies that have a presence in the US and/or a substantial body of American shareholders, as is the case with BP. Quarterly reporting is the norm in the US, though not in the UK.

In fact, there has been a move away from quarterly reporting in the UK because it has encouraged company executives to take a very short term view. If you have to face the wrath of the shareholders every three months it is difficult to plan sensibly for the longer term.

Secondly, a company will have to issue statements for an odd number of months if it decides to change its financial year end. There was once a bit of a fashion for doing this but mercifully it rarely happens these days. It does make comparisons with previous years rather messy.

Two reports each year

For the purposes of this book we shall assume two sets of results per year, especially as the basic principles are equally valid whatever the period covered.

Half yearly figures

The half year figures used to be known as the *interims*. Now that the European Union insists on interim management statements, which are essentially trading updates, we now talk about the *half yearly figures* to avoid confusion.

Preliminary results

The full year figures are known as the *preliminary results* (or *prelims*). Do not be deceived by the name: these are the real thing. Technically the full year results are published in the annual report but the figures are issued through an official news channel as soon as they are ready (otherwise there would be massive scope for insider trading while the annual report was at the printers).

Results when first issued may be *audited* or *unaudited*. You should not worry too much if the statement says the figures are unaudited. Indeed, it is normal for half year figures to be unaudited, although the full year figures must be audited at some point. It is extremely rare for auditors to refuse to sign off the books, although there is always that slight risk while the figures remain unaudited.

Each report has two parts

There are two parts to each set of results.

1. First we have figures showing all the income and expenditure over the period in question. This used to be known as the *profit and loss account* but is now usually referred to as the **income statement**. Neither name is entirely satisfactory: companies make either a profit or a loss, not both at the same time, and the statement covers expenditure as well as income.

2. Secondly there is the **balance statement**, which shows the state of play at the end of the period. It records the value of the company's assets and the amount of cash it had at one moment in time, the period end.

Although every company will be keeping track of its income and expenditure as it goes along, it does take time to get all the figures together. Larger companies, despite having more to tot up, tend to produce their figures more quickly than smaller ones as they have more financial expertise at their disposal.

Nonetheless, it is the case that results figures are several weeks out of date by the time you see them. They thus lack the immediacy of trading statements. Their importance is that they are real figures; they are what actually happened. Forecasts can go horribly wrong and are in any event subject to revision.

It is not within the scope of this book to instruct investors on how to read income statements and balance sheets. A full basic outline is included in my beginner's guide to the stock market, *Shares Made Simple*. Here we are concerned with understanding and interpreting what companies say alongside the results.

What we should see

What we expect to see is something like this from Concurrent Technology, which makes high-tech computer components for industries such as defence, transport and communications:

Financial Highlights

- Profit before tax of £2,951,603 an increase of 21% (2007: £2,432,973)

- Turnover of £12,619,631 an increase of 19% (2007: £10,565,278)

- (Both turnover and profits stronger in second half of year)

- Gross margins for the year strengthened to 53.0% up from 49.4% last year

- Strong balance sheet: cash of £4.99m with no borrowings

- EPS increased to 3.26 pence (2007: 2.62p)

- Total dividend of 1.30 pence per share for the year

Operational Highlights

- Released 9 new products during the year

- Increased requirement for Concurrent's 3U-sized boards – more attractive to critical military applications

- Particularly strong demand from defence sector

- Continued demand from telecommunications and industrial sector despite economic conditions

- Product design and development key to further expansion – engineering centre in Bangalore fully operational and Concurrent continuing to recruit

- Sales growth occurring this year is likely to be more modest than in 2008, but at this stage we expect our financial performance to be satisfactory. Our existing order book and immediate sales prospects give us confidence for the remainder of this year, and, so far as the future beyond that is concerned, we believe there is an abundance of opportunity, particularly in the defence market in the USA.

- We have announced some important new product launches during the past 12 months and expect that the continuing release of even more new products based on the latest multi-core Intel processors should ensure that we are in an excellent position to take advantage of sales opportunities as they arise.

This is an excellent statement notable for its clarity and it avoids getting bogged down in technical jargon with only a passing reference to specific products.

Important figures

We get the important figures first, the profits and sales, with the previous year's figures in brackets for comparison and the percentage gain. We are told that Concurrent did better in the second half than in the first, which means the improvement is gaining rather than losing momentum.

Gross margins have improved, so we know that the gains in sales have not been achieved at the expense of cutting profit margins. Concurrent has cash to fund the business and no borrowings so it can go ahead without worrying about whether it has the continuing support of its bankers.

Figure 5.1: Concurrent Technology

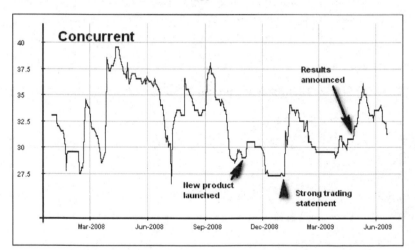

Earnings per share cover the dividend more than twice so the company is being prudent and the payout looks secure even if the sales and profit improvement hits a temporary setback. Indeed, there looks to be scope for an increased dividend even if the next year shows less progress.

We are told that new products have been launched, with more to come, and where the demand is strongest. We finally have a slightly cautious outlook but this statement rings with confidence and we can feel that Concurrent is being prudent.

Missing link

The results statement will normally begin with a series of bullet points highlighting the main points in the statement. Always bear in mind that these pointers, although extremely useful, may put the best gloss on the situation so do not just look at these.

Look at highlights from lighting components maker Dialite:

> Dialight consists of two business segments:
>
> 1. Signals/Illumination which includes Traffic and Rail Signals, Obstruction Lights and Solid State Lighting
>
> 2. Components comprising Light Emitting Diode ("LED") Indication Components and Electromagnetic Disconnects ('smart' meter disconnect switches)
>
> *Highlights*
>
> - Signals/Illumination sales up 30%
>
> - Group sales up 23%
>
> - Operating Profit up 37% to £5.3m – in line with market expectations
>
> - Profit before tax up 26% to £5.6m
>
> - Earnings per share up 27% to 11.2p (2007: 8.8p)
>
> - Strong operating cash flow of £6m (2007: £5.8m)
>
> - The recommended final dividend increased to 3.9 pence

Spot the missing line.

We have sales figures for only one of the two halves of the business. Since group sales have increased by less than those for signals and illuminations we can work out that sales for LED must have done much less well so they don't go into the highlights.

Case study: Thorntons

Let us commend chocolates maker and retailer Thorntons for issuing half yearly figures that were commendably clear despite being on the whole disappointing. Few companies would flag up the deterioration of sales in their own stores when it would have been so easy to stress the sales increases through other stores, on line and by direct marketing.

> The Company delivered an overall sales increase of 1.3%. Sales increases were reported from three of its four sales channels but own stores sales declined during a period in which High Street trading conditions deteriorated.
>
> • Revenues of £128.4 million showed an increase of 1.3% (2008: £126.7 million)
>
> • Profit before tax decreased by 39.0% to £7.3 million (2008: £11.9 million)
>
> • Underlying earnings per share of 7.5p were down 39.6% (2008: 12.5p); reported EPS was adversely impacted by a one-off deferred tax charge of £2.9 million relating to capital allowances
>
> • Net debt increased by £5.0 million to £16.3 million against the same period last year
>
> • The Board has decided to reduce the interim dividend to 1.2 pence per share in line with the decline in underlying earnings

Chocolates sell around Valentine's Day and at Easter so they are not dependent entirely on the Christmas period. Nonetheless, December is a very important month so trends then have a major impact on full year results.

Thorntons chooses to have its year end in July. This has the advantage of putting the half year and full year ends into comparatively quiet periods and eliminates distortions year-on-year from, for example, the timing of Easter. However, it means that the biggest selling period, Christmas, falls in the first half so we should take more note of the interims than we might otherwise do. Most seasonal companies such as tour operators and gardening centres put the stronger period in the second half.

Sales overall are up a little, but not dramatically so the scope for a big sales boost in the full year is heavily dependent on Easter this time.

Thorntons put the sharp decline in profits as its second bullet point. This is uncomfortable reading but it does give the impression that Thorntons is not trying to hide unpleasant truths. Likewise the admission that earnings per share are well adrift and that net debt is higher.

Watch the dividend

Perhaps it is a case of shareholders being softened up for news that the interim dividend is being reduced to 1.2p. A pity that the company could not go one step further and say what from, but your own research will soon tell you that Thorntons paid an interim dividend of 1.95p (the information is buried in the notes at the bottom of the statement which is too long to print in full here).

This is a reduction of 38.5% and it is reasonable to assume that unless sales and profits pick up significantly the final dividend will be cut by a similar amount.

Chief Executive Mike Davies offered some useful pointers to what had gone wrong. It seems that Thorntons got caught up in the High Street battle to slash prices before rather than after Christmas in order to offset a slump in chocolate buying. Davies said:

> Profit was adversely affected by increased promotional activity in response to rapid market decline during the second quarter. Steps were taken to reduce non-discretionary costs, although their impact in the half year was limited.
>
> Thorntons' focus on customer service combined with our strong operational platform and initiatives to reduce operating costs position us well to take advantage of opportunities to improve performance in the second half of the financial year. These include

a three week longer selling season due to a late Easter, increased selling opportunities following the closure of Woolworths and improved productivity versus last year when we incurred higher costs due to the early Easter.

In the longer term we also expect to see benefits arising from improved deals in the property market at the time of lease renewals.

With prudent cost management, product innovation and keeping customers at the forefront of our thinking, I am confident that we will emerge from the current conditions a stronger, more profitable business.

Promotional activity includes such gimmicks as three for the price of two, money-off coupons and cut price days.

Picking out key points

Meanwhile, attempts to reduce costs failed to offset price reductions. Non-discretionary costs are costs that have to be incurred such as rents and raw materials, as opposed to advertising which is a discretionary cost (because you don't have to advertise). However, it is obvious that non-discretionary costs are much harder to reduce, as you have to persuade someone else, such as your landlord or suppliers, to charge you less.

Do not put too much store by comments such as 'strong operational platform'. The operational platform – whatever that means – was not strong enough to prevent a fall in profits, was it? Being 'well positioned' is another popular phrase with chief executives, perhaps because it says very little. All companies aim to be well positioned to do better but not all succeed.

In the same category comes the phrase: 'putting customers at the forefront' – businesses ought to be doing that automatically rather than regarding it as a matter for comment.

Much more specific is the reference to Easter, which had fallen extremely early in the previous year. The longer gap to push chocolate eggs could well help the second half, especially in comparison with the previous year.

Thorntons hopes to negotiate better terms for its leases. Given the property downturn at the time, this was potentially a realistic hope but optimism should be tempered with the thought that landlords are extremely reluctant to reduce rents and it is harder to bargain once you are in the premises. It can be expensive to move premises and other available outlets may be less well sited.

Just walk through any UK high street and you will see that for some reason best known to themselves landlords would rather see premises stand empty than make concessions to tenants.

In any event, any benefits will take time to feed through and will arise spasmodically as leases come up for renewal.

Thorntons always offers a useful insight into how the four different sales channels have fared:

Own Stores

Like-for-like sales in our own stores suffered from the widely reported reduction in footfall on the High Street from mid October to mid December and from the very high level of discounting prevalent from most retailers during that time. Thorntons' policy of offering discounts, in line with other retailers, meant that all Christmas stock was cleared before the end of the period.

Our new own store EPOS system was successfully implemented before Christmas and contributed to improving customer service by significantly reducing transaction times and therefore queuing.

Franchise

Franchise sales increased by 3.7% to £9.9m in the half year, benefiting from the same innovation as our own stores and from increased distribution – we added a net nine new franchise stores during the period increasing the number of stores to 261.

Commercial

Commercial sales grew by 8.9% to £32.4m despite the loss of the Woolworths business. For perspective the Woolworths business represented £4.6m sales during the full year in 2007/08 with over 60% in the first half. The difficulties faced by Woolworths were anticipated and our receivables were well managed, resulting in a small bad debt of £150,000 when Woolworths went into administration.

Thorntons Direct

Sales to consumers, either through our call centre or website, continue to perform well, driven in particular by our customer-friendly website where sales are up 26% versus last year.

Unfortunately our corporate sales to companies that use our products as gifts for their employees or customers have declined as most companies reduce any discretionary spend due to the credit crunch.

The overall impact has been modest growth of 1.3% for total Thorntons Direct sales but margins have improved by 1.5%.

Third party sales

The reference to Woolworths is intriguing. It is true that Thorntons has more opportunity to sell through its own branches following the demise of Woolworths, a major chocolates retailer, but it did sell £4.6 million of Thornton's chocolates a year so this is hardly helpful.

At least some of the Woolworths sales are likely to be lost and it will take time to discover the extent of the damage. Woolworths collapsed in the middle of December so most of the Christmas sales should have been achieved this time.

However, sales to other third party retailers have done remarkably well, more than making up for any loss of sales through Woolworths in the latest period. It has been a recurring theme at Thorntons over the years that other retailers seem to be better at selling Thorntons chocolates than Thorntons' own shops!

To the company's credit, it did minimise the effects of the Woolworths closure by limiting bad debts. While there was plenty of notice that Woolworths was in trouble, its suppliers had to balance the desire to continue to maximise sales without ending up giving its products away. Thorntons seems to have got the balance reasonably right.

Sales through the website are growing rapidly but Thorntons does not, in this statement, give a breakdown of sales figures. You have to go back to its previous update issued seven weeks earlier to confirm that online sales are still a tiny part of the business, accounting for less than 5% of the group total.

Figure 5.2: Thorntons

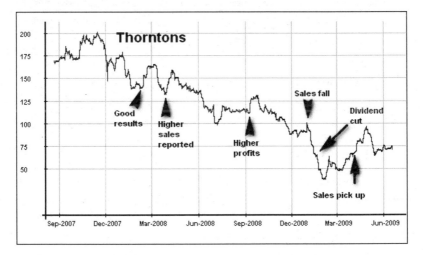

Dig deeper

The importance of looking beyond the bare figures and checking out the background was demonstrated at UK Coal, ostensibly the last vestige of a once proud British industry but recently more profitable as a property company, selling and developing land no longer in production:

UK COAL

Preliminary Financial Results for Year Ended December 2008

- Average coal sales price up 18.5% to £1.92/GJ
- Value of property portfolio resilient
- New/amended coal supply contracts on improved terms
- Significantly increased cash flow for 2009

Financial Highlights

- Total sales up 19.5% to £392.5m reflecting higher average realised coal sales price
- Operating profit pre non-trading exceptionals and pre property revaluation £1.8m (2007: £5.3m)
- Non-cash property revaluation profit £23k (2007: £66.8m)
- Loss before tax £(15.6m) (2007: £69.0m)

Mining and Power

- Production 7.9m tonnes (2007: 7.9mt) Deep mines 6.2mt (2007: 6.4mt). Surface mines 1.7mt (2007: 1.5mt)
- Investments in Kellingley and Thorseby on track to access new areas of reserves at end 2009 and early 2010 respectively
- Will enable improved production rates, costs per tonne and reliability
- Surface mines on track for sustainable 2m tonnes pa production from end 2010

First quarter 2009 production in line with 2008 at 1.7mt

New Coal Contracts

- New/amended contracts with Drax, EON, EDF Energy and Scottish and Southern Energy – a new customer
  - Significantly improved long-term contracted selling prices
  - Immediate cash flow benefits – 2009 c.£85m; 2010 a further c£15m
  - Provides greater certainty and improved economics. Underpins investment programmes

The underlying picture

Note that the top four bullet points are all positive. Look further down and you see that UK Coal recorded a £15.6 million loss in 2008. This was superficially encouraging because the figure was less than a quarter of the previous year's deficit of £69 million but the operating profit tells a different story with a fall from £5.3 million to £1.8 million.

While the pre-tax figure is usually the more important, the operating profit is vital in this case as it gives the underlying picture when there are many distorting factors such as profits on revaluing property.

However, for once the profit figures were not the most important part of the announcement.

Sales are up even though the total amount of coal produced is unchanged, reflecting higher prices that will, if maintained, help profitability and could make some currently uneconomic seams worth opening.

(GJ, by the way, stands for gigajoules, a measurement of energy. As with all forms of mining, it is not just the quantity that is produced but the quality that matters. Measuring the coal by energy produced rather than the quantity gives a more accurate picture. Even if you do not understand the technical term you can at least comprehend the 18.5% increase in prices.)

Although production is unchanged, more coal has come from opencast mines where coal is easier and cheaper to get at. Opencast production is set to increase, again helping future profitability.

This statement came out just after the Government gave the go-ahead for four new coal-fired power stations with new technology to reduce pollution. This is a key factor in the new, more favourable contracts with existing and one new customer.

Figure 5.3: UK Coal

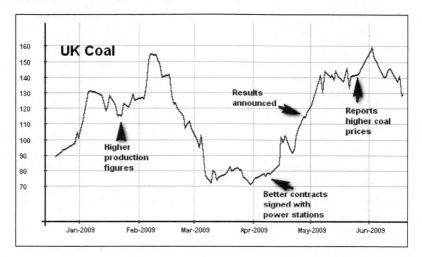

Current investment in two coal fields will help UK Coal to meet these contracts, while cash from the contracts will fund further investment. This kind of virtuous spiral was just the confidence booster that UK Coal needed after years of decline in the industry and the news pushed the shares up from 106p to 115p.

Property companies

Most company results fall into a fairly straightforward template but some sectors can be more tricky. For instance, results from property companies can be difficult to understand because of the different strands to their business:

- Putting up new buildings costs money over a period of time but promises revenue some way into the future.

- Buying existing properties costs more money immediately but produces immediate revenue from rents.

- Managing properties for other investors brings in steady revenue without the capital cost.

- Selling property produces an immediate, usually large, one-off gain but eliminates further revenue in future years.

It follows that the profits of individual property companies can fluctuate enormously, even in years where the state of the property market generally has changed little, depending on the activities of the company during the period under review.

Property sales can boost profits in a particular financial year but these may not be repeated in the following 12 months, which superficially causes a sharp decline in profits from one year to the next when in fact the company may actually have put in a better performance overall.

A revaluation of property owned by the company can create a one-off profit or loss, especially as property revaluations tend to be carried out every three years rather than annually.

Also, results are seriously affected if a property company invests mainly in one type of property. For example, office buildings may be in demand while the residential market slumps, or warehousing may be stagnating while shopping centres boom.

Valuing assets

Property companies will give a net asset value per share when they announce their results. This gives an indication of what the company is worth but, even if it is shown as adjusted and diluted (to allow for the subsequent sale or purchase of property and the possible issuing of new shares) it tends to give a slightly inflated view of the company's true worth.

Triple net asset value

So a rather complicated calculation known as triple net asset value has been concocted as a commonly accepted method of valuing a property company's portfolio. You take the theoretical market value of the company's assets but deduct items such as continuing development costs, borrowings and tax to be paid to get a more accurate valuation as things actually stand.

You divide the figure by the number of shares issued to get a valuation per share. Tripling the figure gives a rough and ready guide to what the share price should be on the stock market.

This sounds highly theoretical but it does work pretty well.

Property developers' shares tend to trade at a slight premium to triple net asset value to allow for a supposed increase in values between the date of the valuation and the timing of the results announcement plus an allowance for the expected continued rise in values over the following months.

A discount to the valuation implies either that property values are falling or that the company's shares are undervalued. If you are thinking of investing in a property company it is worth checking whether the sector generally is on a premium or a discount, and on the size of the gap between triple net asset value per share and the actual share price of each company, to get a feel for the overall state of the market.

It is not necessary to fully understand the complicated calculations but it is important to remember that triple net asset is the best indication of where the shares should be.

Debt levels

Another point worth noting is that debt tends to fluctuate considerably and can be frighteningly large. This is an inevitable consequence of the cost of constructing large developments and of the buying and selling of property.

Wheeler-dealing is quite common in the sector as property developers take differing views on how high the yield (that is the rental return as a percentage of the price of the property) should be.

A high debt level is not necessarily a cause for concern in a property company; nor should a sharp rise in debt in itself set off alarm bells. However, it does mean that property companies are at risk when credit is tight or interest rates are high.

Case study: Terrace Hill

Terrace Hill is a property company that has grown from small beginnings, showing over the years a knack of being in the right place at the right time and an ability to miss the worst of the downturns on various property sectors through an astute policy of buying and selling land and buildings.

Even so, it could not buck the severe property slump, as figures for the year to 31 October, 2008, show. Terrace Hill figures highlight the need to distinguish between regular income and large one-off gains together with shifts in asset values, which are valuations on paper rather than immediate tangible gains.

Commendably, it makes clear the difference between the overall state of the business (the financial highlights) and the performance over the previous 12 months (operational highlights).

Financial highlights

- Triple Net Asset Value per share of 53.4p (31 October 2007: 83.7p)

- Adjusted Diluted Net Asset Value per share of 58.0p
  (31 October 2007: 96.3p)

- £108.2 million of debt refinanced since October 2007

- Adjusted pre-tax profit (before property provisions) £1.0 million
  (31 October 2007: £4.7 million)

- Pre-tax loss of £31.6 million (31 October 2007: profit
  £18.1 million)

- Balance sheet loan to value gearing of 45.7%

- Final dividend of 0.54 pence per share, bringing the total dividend for the year to 1.34 pence per share, demonstrating the Board's confidence in the Company's financial strength and long-term prospects

- Sale of Queens Wharf, Hammersmith, completed for
  £30.75 million realising a profit of £11.1 million

Remembering that shares normally trade at a slight premium to triple net asset value, you would expect Terrace Hill shares to have fallen from about 85p a year earlier to about 55p.

Figure 5.4: Terrace Hill

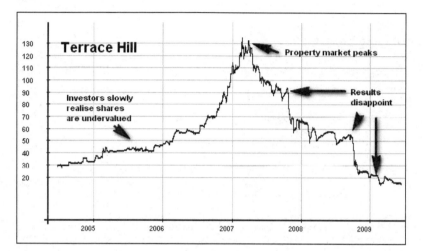

Some five years earlier when Terrace Hill shares were at a discount to triple net asset value it was indeed a signal to buy. The shares shot up from under 40p to over 100p. However, in the depths of the credit crunch it was sensible to be cautious about property companies and a discount was understandable.

Note that the adjusted diluted net asset value per share would have given a more exaggerated and less realistic view of Terrace Hill.

Debt dwarfs annual profits but it has at least been refinanced (that is the banks have agreed to lend for a longer term, in the teeth of the credit crunch). Loan to value gearing indicates that Terrace Hill's borrowings are just under half the value of its assets.

We can see from the profits figures that Terrace Hill has done less well in the most recent period compared with the previous 12 months. In particular, a reduction of the value of the property portfolio at a time of falling property prices has had a hefty impact on the pre-tax figure, but even adjusting for this setback we can see that profits are down by nearly 80%.

At least there is the encouragement of a large property sale in London at a profit and there is a dividend.

Staying alert to opportunities

To get some ideas of recent and forthcoming events, Terrace Hill provides a summary which shows it remains active and alive to opportunities:

Operational highlights

- Completed or contracted sales of £72.4 million

- Contracted lettings with annual rent roll of £5.7 million

- Gained detailed planning consent for 882,155 sq ft

- Pre-let a 92,333 sq ft superstore in Bishop Auckland to Sainsbury's and contracted to sell a five-acre site to them in Helston

- Planning applications submitted at four Scottish housebuilding sites for a total of 519 units

This does, however, have to be seen in the context of the overall economic situation. Commenting, Robert Adair, Chairman of Terrace Hill, said:

> In line with the rest of the sector, our financial results are, of course, greatly affected by the general economic situation. As a result, we have seen a fall in trading margins and volumes, increased funding costs and falls in triple net asset value as a result of asset value writedowns.
>
> Clearly the immediate future for our industry looks challenging and I anticipate further falls in asset values.

So the situation is tough and is going to get tougher. Investors were thus warned that the fall in the share price was likely to continue.

6.
AGMs

The holding of an annual general meeting (a legal requirement for a quoted company) can be an excellent source of information.

Most AGMs are favoured with some indication of current trading. This can range from a mundane expression of platitudes with a rehash of what is already in the public domain to a full trading update complete with the latest sales figures.

It is much better, if you are a shareholder and can get to the venue, to attend the AGM because you and other shareholders have the opportunity to cross-examine the directors. You can see first-hand whether they are on top of the game or wriggling on a hook.

Fortunately, the trend has been for AGM statements to be increasingly meaningful and informative.

It may also be possible to glean information at an EGM but this is less likely to be a source of useful information because:

- EGMs are often held immediately before or after the AGM to avoid the expense of two separate meetings.

- EGMs have a specific item or items of business, such as approving a rights issue.

- A trading update may well have already been issued when the EGM was called as part of the explanation of why the meeting is needed.

AGMs also have a specific business agenda but they are much wider ranging in nature and, as they are the one opportunity per year that the owners of the business have to confront the directors, even the most evasive chairman is put to the test.

If you hold shares in a company you will have been notified of the time and place of the meeting. The information will be contained in the annual report, which is posted to you.

If you are thinking of investing in a company you can get a good idea of when the AGM will be held by looking on the company's website to see when it was held in the previous year. It is likely to be held within a day or two of the same date the following year.

Chairman's statement

Whether you intend to attend it or not, it is always worth checking if the chairman's statement has been issued in advance, which has the merit of treating all shareholders equally, irrespective of whether they can make the annual get-together. The statement will be released through the RNS at 7am before stock market trading starts.

Sometimes, however, the statement is released immediately after the meeting. This is less satisfactory as you cannot be sure what time the meeting will finish.

As with all such statements, it is worth reading to the bottom as:

- The preamble to the statement may be pure waffle.

- The chairman is human and will wish to put the positive side of things first.

- Really bad news may be hidden by a chairman who has to face the wrath of shareholders that day.

Case study: Mitchells & Butlers

Everything in the pub garden appeared lovely on the day of the annual general meeting. As is usual, the statement was issued through the stock exchange at 7am, rather than waiting for the meeting to start at 11am.

The pubs group issued a bullish trading statement with these highlights:

- Resilient like-for-like sales up 1.0% in the 9 weeks to 24 January
- Accelerating market share gains
- Strong cash flow with £52m of disposals agreed to date
- Uplifts of over 20% in sales from newly converted ex-Whitbread sites
- Overall results in line with Board's expectations

While these bullet points all sounded positive, they were on closer inspection a mixed bag. Beware of the word 'resilient'. It implies that the company is struggling to hold its own while its markets are shrinking.

An increase in like-for-like sales is commendable but 1% is hardly dramatic and could be more than accounted for by an increase in prices.

It is good to see that M&B is gaining business from competitors but if comparable sales are only 1% ahead then it does not look like much of a gain. It is possible that weaker competitors who are losing market share will eventually go to the wall, leaving more business for M&B, but that will take time.

Strong cash flow is also desirable, particularly during a credit crunch, but it seems that the cash has come from disposals rather than from the business itself. Cash flow from disposals comes to an end when there is nothing left to sell.

The best line among the bullet points is that sales at sites acquired from another group are very strong. Money has been spent buying these pubs and refurbishing them. It is important that they pay for themselves from the word go, which is what appears to be happening.

Finally we learn that results overall are in line with the board's expectations. You must decide for yourself whether the glass is half full or half empty. Trading has not improved particularly since the company's last pronouncement but nor are there any nasty surprises.

In this case it is, on balance, a positive factor. There were concerns about trading in the key Christmas period given the parlous state of the economy at the time. M&B has come through pretty much unscathed.

What the chairman said

The chairman's enthusiastic comments, to be presented to the meeting itself, followed the bullet points:

Current Trading

The pattern of trading since the Preliminary results update on 26 November saw a slow build up in early December followed by a strong two week Christmas period. January trading has been resilient amidst a challenging market.

Amidst a weakening eating-out market, like-for-like food sales growth in the first 17 weeks of 2.6% remains robust. Our ability to utilise our scale advantages to deliver quality offers at good value, such as the £3.50 main meal price in Crown Carveries or the £4.99 Harvester Earlybird offer, is generating profitable volume growth with strong associated drinks sales. Moreover, drinks sales growth continues to strengthen with like-for-like drinks sales up 1.2% in the first 17 weeks. Against an on-trade drinks market in serious decline with UK beer volumes down 9.9% in the three months to the end of December 2008, this represents our strongest ever recorded rate of market share gain.

These assurances are, on the whole, encouraging. Trading has if anything gathered momentum over the latest period, with a slow start followed by gains.

While the downturn in the market, particularly beer sales, is spelt out clearly, one feels that M&B has a clear strategy that is, on the whole, working. Remember, in any sector there will be those doing better than others whether circumstances are easy or difficult. The trick for investors is to spot which companies offer the best prospects.

The chairman offered guidance on the immediate future:

Outlook

Recessionary pressures are intensifying, and as a result we expect continued sizable declines in on-trade beer volumes and a significant contraction in the eating out market. Against this adverse demand background, the quality of our pubs and their value for money positioning underpin our confidence of a further increase in the rate of market share gains.

As previously disclosed, cost pressures continue to be substantial with £20m of regulatory cost increases and some £30m of food and energy cost increases which are heavily concentrated in the first half. However, forward cost prices in the second half for energy and food are starting to see declines, although these markets remain volatile. To mitigate the cost pressures, we expect to realise some £20m of cost savings in the year.

Overall, despite the challenges from weakening consumer demand and the cost pressures, the quality of our well invested estate, the value and volume sales strategy, further cost efficiencies and the opportunities for accelerated market share gains are set to support a resilient trading performance amidst recessionary economic conditions.

So, the market was tough but M&B was well on top of its game, the message implied. Nor was there any clear hint of a problem in the statement issued after the AGM giving the voting figures at the meeting:

The results of polls on resolutions 1 to 6 and 8 to 12 were passed by the required majority, resolution 7 did not receive the required majority of votes.

Then followed a table of the voting figures:

Resolution		Votes For (Note)*	Votes Against	Total Votes
1.	Report & Accounts	124,476,875	828,802	125,305,677
2.	Remuneration Report	123,315,232	89,178,866	212,494,098
3(a)	Reappointment of Tim Clarke	126,750,818	436,390	127,187,208
3(b)	Reappointment of Sir Tim Lankester	124,639,522	1,183,816	125,823,338
3(c)	Reappointment of Jeremy Townsend	126,789,686	394,137	127,183,823
4.	Reappointment of Auditors	125,697,405	974,456	126,671,861
5.	Auditors' Remuneration	126,625,234	998,744	127,623,978
6.	Allotment of Shares	113,980,332	101,614,245	215,594,577
7.	Disapplication of Pre-Emption Rights**	113,482,636	101,642,837	215,125,473
8.	Authority to Purchase Own Shares**	127,475,431	159,454	127,634,885
9.	Political Donations	111,880,614	15,563,442	127,444,056
10.	Borrowing Powers**	127,343,515	202,421	127,545,936
11.	Articles of Association**	127,507,421	84,760	127,592,181
12.	Notice Period for Extraordinary General Meetings**	124,093,414	1,202,492	125,295,906
Notes:				
*The "For" vote includes those giving the Chairman discretion **Special resolutions				

In fact, there had been a major shareholder revolt. It is rare indeed for the board of any quoted company to lose any vote at a meeting of shareholders and the directors did gain more than half the votes for each resolution put to the meeting. However, a sizeable vote against the board is worth noting.

What the figures show

A close scrutiny of the voting figures showed that nearly half of votes cast had opposed allowing the board to issue shares worth up to 33% of the share capital (resolution 6) and against allowing the board to issue shares to outsiders without having to offer existing shareholders the right to buy them (resolution 7). Because special resolutions require a 75% vote in favour, resolution 7 failed.

There was also a substantial though lower vote against the remuneration report (resolution 2) which sets directors' pay.

These three resolutions attracted a much higher total vote than the other less contentious issues. Nevertheless, it was clear that the rebels had declined to vote for any resolutions, a further show of dissent.

The AGM was held early in 2009 at a time when share placings and rights issues were being contemplated by a wide range of companies, either to reduce debt or to take business opportunities while rivals were weak – indeed, several companies including explorer Tullow Oil, reinsurer Chaucer Holdings and property group Helical Bar – had already made such a move.

M&B's largest shareholder, Joe Lewis, voted against the relevant resolutions to prevent the pub chain from diluting his 25% holding.

None of this was explained in the company's statement. Nor was it obliged to offer any explanation. In these circumstances shareholders and potential investors may be obliged to find out in the following day's newspapers. In this case it appeared that several other large shareholders with 16% between them sided with Lewis.

Figure 6.1: Mitchells & Butlers

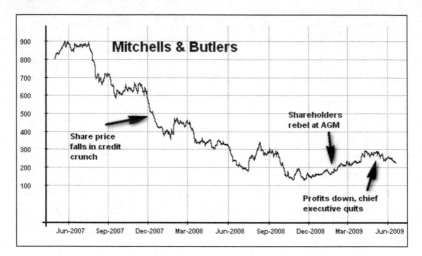

Caution is always warranted where there is a shareholder revolt so always check the voting figures just to be sure. A company at war with its major shareholders is bad news. At the very least, the board may be distracted by efforts to make peace. In an extreme case it could be an indication that the board has lost its way.

Section C – One-off Statements

7.

Alerts

Sudden, sharp movements in a particular company's share price are quite commonplace. The market is rife with rumours, some true and some false. It is virtually impossible for investors to determine at first sight whether a leap or slump in a share is due to fact or fiction.

Over time it probably works out 50:50 whether share price movements are based on fact or fiction. When there is plenty of action it is harder for rumours to attract attention, while quiet weeks or months give greater scope for idle tongues.

Sometimes, despite the best endeavours of the regulators to maintain a level playing field, news of some major development leaks out. This is usually when a takeover bid is in the offing: too many people need to know about it to gag everyone.

Unfortunately, less scrupulous investors take advantage of the fact that rumours sometimes turn out to be true. They peddle credible reports, often on website bulletin boards, to drive prices so that they can dump stock or buy in cheaply.

As with the rumour mongers, the press sometimes gets it right and sometimes wrong. Press comment is particularly potent in those sectors selling directly to the public, such as retailers, where spending patterns can change dramatically over a few months or even weeks and companies are constantly comparing sales now with those of a year ago. Even if nothing is leaked from the companies concerned, newspapers can speculate on who is buying what on the High Street.

Companies are obliged to offer clarification when the share price moves substantially. There is no set figure for what constitutes a substantial movement, although 10% is widely regarded as the norm. Quoted companies are, on the whole, pretty conscientious in keeping the market informed and they can be prompted to do the decent thing by the stock exchange if necessary.

False alarms

In many cases, companies are as baffled as shareholders by a sudden share price movement. In these cases the ensuing statement will be to the point, as is this one from Alecto Energy, which invests in energy projects.

Share price movement

Alecto Energy has noted the recent movement in its share price and confirms that the Board is not aware of any reason for this movement.

Alecto is a curious case of how companies these days err on the side of making announcements even when nothing much is happening. (The share price, which had barely risen above 3p since the company joined AIM in 2006, sunk to a measly 0.03p when it suddenly trebled to 0.1p!)

To the point

As an example of getting to the point, this offering from property developer Eatonfield is what we want:

Statement re share price increase

The Directors of Eatonfield note the recent substantial increase in the Company's share price and wish to notify the market that they are not aware of any reason for such a movement. The Directors are also satisfied that all information of a price-sensitive nature has previously been notified to the market.

Full marks to Eatonfield for making it clear that the share price movement was up rather than down (most companies leave you to check what has happened for yourself) and for the clarity of its statement. *Price sensitive information* means news that could cause the share price to move.

Eatonfield had gone through a torrid patch as property prices fell in the credit crunch and its shares had slumped from a peak of 188p to a measly 2.5p in little over a year. Then, within the space of three days, they shot up to 25p, ten times their previous value.

The denial that anything was afoot eventually brought them back to 14p but that took several hours and alert shareholders had the chance to get out if they wished at a higher price in the meantime.

When one talks of a sharp movement in a company's share price caused by press reports one tends to think of scare stories. However, reports can drive share prices up as well as down.

Case study: Thomas Cook

Travel company Thomas Cook was one case of a share price being moved by press reports, although one has to say that its response to favourable comment was a masterpiece of divulging nothing:

> **Thomas Cook notes the recent press comment and share price movement**
>
> Thomas Cook notes that the performance of the Group overall continues to be in line with the performance outlined at the time of releasing its Interim Management Statement on 12 February 2009. Whilst the market continues to be challenging, the Board remains confident in achieving its expectations for the year as a whole and believes that the Group remains well positioned for the future.

Phrases such as 'the market continues to be challenging' and 'well positioned for the future' are pretty meaningless. The only thing we have to go on here is the fact that nothing has apparently changed since Cook issued a trading update about a month earlier.

A check back to the previous pronouncement showed that it had been somewhat downbeat. Cook had said that bookings were well down on the previous year and it was reaching its financial targets only because it had reduced capacity.

The travel company had also warned that it was struggling with higher fuel bills as it had fixed prices on its supplies up to 14 months in advance, so it was not benefiting from recent falls in the price of crude oil.

Analysts had calculated that the company needed to increase prices by 6% in the UK to cover fuel costs and offset the fall in the value of the pound.

Investors had to choose between Cook's indication that the tourist industry was suffering in the credit crunch or believing press reports suggesting that holiday bookings for the following summer were improving. In these circumstances the market will generally accept the company line.

Figure 7.1: Thomas Cook

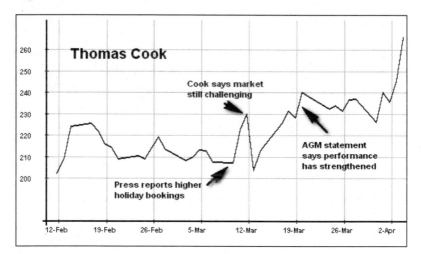

From a low of 130p, the shares had been recovering and they shot up from 208p to 230p on the favourable press comment. Thomas Cook's noncommittal response promptly dragged them back down to 204p.

Frankly, there are no rights and wrongs in his type of situation. Investors must use their own judgement and keep an eye on how the situation develops. In this case the press were vindicated, as Cook proved in its next update:

Despite the challenging trading environment we are pleased the business performance has strengthened.

Winter: The clear trend towards later bookings continues. Despite the distorting impact of a later Easter, bookings have improved significantly in the last four weeks, particularly in our Continental and Northern European segments. Average selling prices are up year on year and load factors on departed flights remain at least at last year's levels.

Summer: Summer trading in the UK has been robust. Cumulative bookings are tracking in line with capacity reductions of 11%, and we have now sold 52% of our capacity, in line with the prior year. Having successfully focused on selling the months on either side of the July/August peak, we now have 14% less left to sell than last year in these shoulder months. Given that mix we are pleased to have driven average selling prices up 9% overall.

Ups and downs

Let us look at two cases where companies were prompted to make unequivocal statements after share price movements, one where the shares when down and the other where shares went up.

In such cases the resulting statement from the company may be quite brief, especially if plans are at an early stage, and will read something like this one from industrial property landlord Brixton:

Response to share price movement

The Board of Brixton notes the recent movement in the Company's share price.

Given the ongoing challenging market conditions in the real estate and financial markets, the Board of Brixton is pursuing a range of options to provide additional financial flexibility, including disposals from its investment portfolio, as well as considering an equity raising. No decision on any course of action has been taken at this stage.

A further announcement will be made as and when appropriate.

Brixton's shares had been on the slide since peaking at 575p at the start of 2007 and the well publicised travails of the property market had pushed them well below 100p by early 2009.

It was a fall of 19p from 67p to 48p – over 28% – on the previous day that prompted the announcement.

Figure 7.2: Brixton

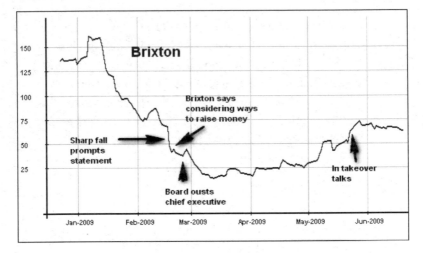

Brixton shares continued on their downward path to 15p three weeks later, by which time the chief executive had been ousted by the rest of the board.

Strategic review

In contrast, healthcare group Claimar Care's prompt reaction was in response to a rise in its share price:

> Claimar Care confirms that it is in the early stages of undertaking a strategic review to consider how best to take the business forward.
>
> The strategic review has been initiated by the Board as it is disappointed with the Company's depressed share price, which it

feels does not fairly reflect the Company's strong market position and growth prospects.

As part of this review, the Claimar Care Board will be considering a number of options available to the Company to maximise shareholder value including the possible sale of all or part of the business, and accordingly has appointed KPMG Corporate Finance as financial advisor to assist with this process.

The strategic review is at a very early stage and the Board intends to update shareholders when appropriate.

Accordingly, under the rules of the Takeover Code, Claimar Care is now in an offer period.

Claimar, which provides care for old people privately and through local councils, had seen its shares slump from 170p in mid-2007 to below 10p a year later. After months of meandering aimlessly they suddenly perked up from 7.25p to 9.25p. Confirmation that something was afoot pushed them back above 10p.

Figure 7.3: Claimar

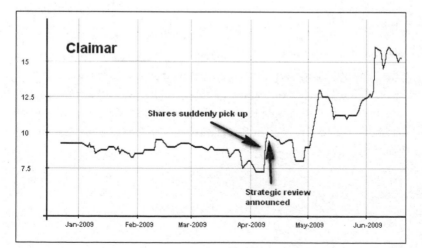

While these are comparatively small figures, they did mean that anyone buying before the announcement turned a nice little profit.

The review could all come to nothing but all options are being kept open. Potential bidders have been alerted to the fact that the company is willing to be taken over and its share price is depressed.

Profit warnings

Not all profit warnings are dire, although they are invariably unwelcome. It is sensible to sift through them with a cautious eye, bearing in mind that management, like the shareholders, are naturally hoping for the best.

Specialist engineering and construction services group Renew began its profit warning thus:

> Results for the first half of the year are expected to be satisfactory, however the outlook has deteriorated and as a result the Board does not now expect the Group's results to meet full year market expectations.

It depends what you mean by 'satisfactory'. The failure of results to meet previous expectations will hardly satisfy investors and it surely doesn't give the directors much pleasure either.

It is true that both building and engineering had been through more than a year of sharp decline before this announcement was made but that is little consolation. The state of the market was well known and had been taken into account in setting out previous expectations on which the share price had been based. There is no getting round the fact that the situation is worse than everyone thought it was.

Separate trading arms

Renew provided some detail on its two trading arms, which helped shareholders to assess the situation. First, specialist building:

> The last two months have been challenging, with project cancellations and deferrals leading to reduced trading expectations for the second half of this financial year. As a result of these weaker market conditions, the Board is acting to reduce capacity in this business stream by a further 23%, giving a reduction of 37% over the last year. These cost reductions will be implemented progressively through the second half of the year.
>
> This action will result in an exceptional charge in the second half of £2.5m for redundancy and other restructuring costs. The resultant savings in annual costs will be more than £7m. The Board believes that this further reduced cost base positions its Specialist Building business appropriately in the current difficult economic climate. The focus in this area will remain on project selectivity and quality of earnings. Operating margins in Specialist Building will decrease reflecting the economic pressures currently prevailing in this market.

So we know that trading in this division has taken a turn for the worst quite recently and Renew is working on the basis that there will be no immediate improvement. Having already reduced capacity in the division it is cutting back even further. It is encouraging that Renew is taking action to mitigate the worsened circumstances but disappointing that past action has been insufficient.

Renew promises to be more picky about the projects it takes on, although that will inevitably reduce turnover. More worrying is the fact that profit margins will still be lower even if Renew concentrates on only the most profitable contracts available, a clear sign of how tough market conditions are.

Reduced capacity means a reduced workforce, so redundancies have to be paid for. It will take time for the savings in wages to offset the redundancy costs.

Now for specialist engineering:

> The market and the forward order book remain stable with trading for the full year anticipated to be in line with market expectations. Specialist Engineering is expected to represent approximately 40% of Group revenues going forward with operating margins remaining stable.
>
> The Board intends to continue to strengthen and develop its Specialist Engineering activities both organically and by acquisition and can report that C&A Pumps has integrated well into the Group since its acquisition on 1 October 2008.

This is much more encouraging. In fact, many companies would have put the paragraphs about engineering above the building side in the announcement to present the better news first.

Engineering is the smaller half of the business, which is a shame, but it is growing and the latest acquisition has fitted in well.

Legacy issues

There is one further matter in the statement:

> The Group has recently reached final account settlement on the last of the basket of legacy construction contracts, which were originally provided against in 2005. This has led to an exceptional charge of £1m which will be reported in the first half results.

Legacy issues are always bad news. They crop up when some disaster has befallen and it takes a number of years to sort out who is to pay to sort out the mess. One notable example was construction group Jarvis, which tendered for contracts then found that it had undercharged. Losses were recorded until all the projects were completed. Other examples elsewhere have been meeting compensation claims from smokers who developed cancer and removing asbestos from buildings constructed before the dangers were realised.

Legacy issues can hang as a pall over a company so the settlement of problem contracts is a cause for relief, even if it has cost £1m more than Renew originally set aside.

Read to the end

The final paragraph was vital – always read to the end of the statement:

> Renew's balance sheet remains debt free with substantial cash resources and the Board intends to declare an unchanged interim dividend of 1.0p per share.

It appears that, in difficult circumstances, the situation is under control and that we should give the Renew directors the benefit of the doubt. At least there will be no bank calling in loans or demanding higher interest payments. And there is enough leeway to maintain the dividend, another plus point. Shareholders should bear in mind that the dividend could still be reduced later if trading conditions get worse.

However, a look back over past years' trading puts the present difficulties into context. Renew has been a prudent company, as its lack of debt indicates. Despite the difficulties in the construction industry, it grew profits strongly in the four years to 30 September 2008.

The dividend had increased in those years but the 2.2p paid in the most recent 12-month period was covered 5.6 times by earnings, which provides plenty of leeway. In fact, house broker Brewin Dolphin was forecasting a dividend for the current financial year of 3p, which would be covered more than twice even if profits were halved.

Figure 7.4: Renew

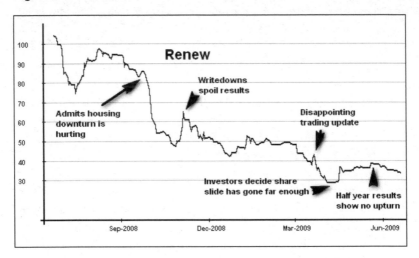

Renew shares had already fallen from 114p a year earlier to 43p when the profit warning was issued and they tumbled to 35p immediately after. Investors studying the announcement were entitled to consider whether the fall had been overdone.

Case study: Cattles

Apparently routine announcements can be much more important than they look on the surface, as a seemingly innocuous announcement from Cattles turned out to be.

Cattles is mainly a money lending operation, its Welcome Finance arm concentrating on the sub-prime end of the UK market, with higher risk customers such as those who are self-employed or have previously defaulted on loan repayments.

As Cattles puts it, they are:

> non-standard customers, individuals who may currently not have access to mainstream facilities – typically due to perceived shortcomings in their employment, residency or credit histories.

Welcome also provided finance for buying new and used cars.

The other parts of the business were the Lewis Group, a debt collecting agency that bought up bad debt from other lenders as well as chasing Cattle's own recalcitrant borrowers, and Cattles Invoice Finance providing working capital for small and medium businesses. These two arms were, however, only a tiny part of the Cattles group in terms of turnover and profits.

Given that the credit crunch was sparked by lending to sub-prime borrowers, the Cattles business model was to be viewed by investors as suspect in the difficult financial climate. If banks had got into trouble lending to borrowers who might not pay up, investors were entitled to worry what sort of risks Cattles was taking.

It transpired that Cattles was, in fact, sensibly trying to lesson its risks by seeking a banking licence to take deposits but it met with no success as the following announcement showed:

Cattles withdraws its application for permission to take retail deposits

Over recent weeks Cattles has been in discussions with the Financial Services Authority regarding its application for permission to take retail deposits. Following the most recent discussions, it has become clear that permission is unlikely to be forthcoming until the unprecedented turmoil in the financial markets has stabilised and the terms of the Group's renegotiation of £635 million of its bank facilities are known. Given these circumstances, the Group has decided to withdraw its application until such a time as there is greater clarity on both these matters.

Cattles and its lending banks continue to have constructive discussions about the scope and terms of the renewal of the Group's bank facilities which are due this year. Cattles' proposals to its banks do not include any reliance on funding from retail deposits. Cattles will provide a further update on the progress of these discussions by the end of the first quarter of this year.

> David Postings, Chief Executive of Cattles, said: 'Given the turmoil in the financial markets we have taken prompt and prudent action to reduce costs, conserve capital and to focus our efforts on securing ongoing wholesale funding for the Group. Demand for our products remains strong and the Group continues to trade profitably and in line with expectations.'

On the credit side …

In fairness to Cattles, one has to say that it had performed exceptionally well in the circumstances. One might have expected it to collapse first when the credit crunch struck but it remained remarkably resilient while larger institutions such as Northern Rock and HBOS had gone to the wall.

The chief executive was able to point out that Cattles had continued to trade profitably throughout the earlier stages of the crisis. The company even persuaded shareholders to put up £209m in a successful rights issue in 2008 in the hope of ensuring that it had sufficient capital to meet stricter regulatory rules.

Nonetheless, shareholders needed to be on their guard and Cattles had announced plans to:

> reduce costs, preserve liquidity and strengthen the capital position of the business during the course of 2009.

… on the debit side

The problem was that Cattles relied on a syndicate of banks to provide the cash that it lent on to individual customers at higher rates. These loans were coming up for renewal in six months time and members of the lending syndicate had problems of their own. It was likely that at least some would refuse to renew the arrangement; possibly they would all demur.

Thus Cattles was in an ominously similar position to the one Northern Rock had found itself in a year earlier: its source of funds was likely to dry up, making it impossible to continue lending.

Within a month of withdrawing its application for a retail banking licence, this worrying admission came:

> The Board of Cattles Plc announces a delay in the release of its Preliminary Results announcement pending completion of a review of the adequacy of its impairment provisions. Although it is not possible to determine the outcome of the review at this stage, it is expected to result in profit before tax being substantially lower than current market expectations. A new date for the results will be released in due course.

The situation at Cattles suddenly had to be seen in a far more serious light. It is rare for a company to defer the release of its results indefinitely; the reason for deferral is almost invariably significant and usually detrimental.

In this case Cattles cites 'the adequacy of its impairment provisions'. In other words, it seems that it has made insufficient provision for bad debts. You would have hoped that, given the financial standing of its borrowers and the scale of the economic downturn, Cattles would have been particularly prudent in this regard.

At least Cattles spells out what the problem is. In this situation we often get euphemisms such as 'pending clarification of its financial position' – which usually means the company is about to go bust.

So at this stage the situation at Cattles is worrying but not necessarily disastrous. The company is still claiming to be in profit even after making more substantial writedowns.

From bad to worse

It is remarkable how often, when things go wrong, they go spectacularly wrong and investors do well to heed the warning signs early. Cattles did not disappoint those who believe that profit warnings always come in threes (or more).

We did not have to wait long for the next signs of unravelling:

Cattles suspends lending to new customers

The Board of Cattles announces that in order to preserve liquidity in the business, it is temporarily suspending lending to new customers in Welcome Finance with immediate effect. Welcome Finance will continue to offer renewal products to existing customers.

The Board has appointed Deloitte, its internal auditor, to assist management in the review of Cattles' impairment provisions which was announced last week.

James Corr, Cattles' Finance Director, who was due to retire at the end of February, will remain in his role until the current review is completed. Accordingly, Robert East's planned appointment to the Board, as Finance Director, has been deferred until further notice.

Welcome was far and away the main party of the business, so the suspension of lending to new customers was a serious blow. Apart from the army of agents who collected repayments on the doorstep, Cattles had 183 branches across the UK, a network that was financed by interest on loans that were being seriously curtailed.

The offering of 'renewal products' was probably an indication that customers who could not pay were having to be allowed to roll over their borrowings into new loans, so even this continuing business offered little help in keeping cash rolling into the depleted Cattles coffers.

A sign of the scale of the difficulties was the postponement of the retirement of the finance director, though one should not put too much emphasis on this in itself. It would be sensible to keep in place the man who knows the books while a full review is conducted. There could be awkward questions that need answering.

Breakdown of internal controls

Deloitte wasted no time getting to grips with the situation (as one would expect given that it already audited the accounts). Within days Cattles issued another statement:

> Based on work carried out to date, the Board believes that there has been a breakdown in internal controls which has resulted in the Group's impairment policies having been applied incorrectly. Although it is still not possible to quantify the effect on the Group's financial statements, the Board believes that profit before tax for the year ended 31 December 2008, is likely to be substantially lower than its expectations as at 20 February, 2009.
>
> The Board anticipates that it will be required to enter into discussions with its banks and the holders of its outstanding Eurobonds and US Private Placement Notes.
>
> David Postings, CEO of Cattles, has taken direct management control of Welcome Financial Services, Cattles' principal operating entity. Mr. John Blake, Managing Director, Mr. Peter Miller, Finance Director and Mr. Mick Belcher, Operations Director of Welcome Financial Services, have been suspended pending the outcome of an inquiry which is also being conducted by Deloitte.

Oh dear. A breakdown in internal controls means that things have been going on that the board doesn't know about. The scope for squandering money, failing to report losses or pretending to have made non-existent profits is considerable and can easily wipe out profits for a whole year.

Such actions may have been done for fraud, to please the bosses, to safeguard middle management jobs or simply to smooth out a dip in sales in the hope that it will all come right in due course.

We do not know yet if the three key Welcome executives have breached Cattles' internal controls or, if they have, what their motives may be. Suffice to say that something went wrong on their watch. Precisely what is of no direct interest to investors, whose main concern is that problems are mounting by the day.

Failure of internal controls often runs for several years and the effects tend to snowball, as ever greater manipulation of accounts is needed to cover up for past indiscretions. Often, as here, the existence and extent of the problem comes to light during a special audit rather than in routine annual audits.

Profit expectations are lowered again and even before the current audit is complete it is clear that Cattles will have to negotiate with the people who have lent it money in euros and US dollars as it will probably breach the terms of the loans. Like the people it lent money to, Cattles has become a bad credit risk.

From profit to loss

Further progress in the financial review was reported a week later:

> Based on information received to date and subject to completion of its external audit, the Board believes that the Group will incur a significant loss before tax for the year ended 31 December, 2008 and that it will be necessary to restate the Group's financial statements for the year ended 31 December, 2007.
>
> The Board believes that Cattles is in breach of covenants under its borrowing arrangements and Cattles will therefore be seeking appropriate waivers from its relevant debt providers.
>
> The Board now announces that Mr. James Corr, Finance Director of Cattles, Mr. Ian Cummine, Chief Operating Officer of Cattles and Chairman of Welcome Financial Services, and Mr. Adrian Cummings, Compliance and Risk Director for Welcome Financial Services Lending Division, have been suspended pending the outcome of the review.

Readers of the previous statements should not be surprised to learn that Cattles, rather than making a profit, is now staring at a loss for the previous year and will have to recalculate its account for the 12 months before that.

Figure 7.5: Cattles

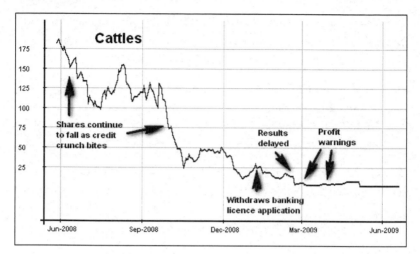

Nor should it come as a shock that the company has broken its banking agreements. Just as Cattles could impose a higher rate of interest on its riskiest customers, so too would its own bankers demand their pound of flesh for continuing the banking arrangements. Alternatively, they could simply pull the plug and put the company into receivership.

Cattles may seek waivers, under which the banks would agree to overlook the breaches of the terms of the loans, but the banks are not obliged to acquiesce.

Three more key executives are suspended, including the finance director who by now had succumbed to illness anyway, leaving the group distinctly short of managerial expertise.

Suspension pending clarification

One statement you hope will never be put out by any company in which you hold shares is short and far from sweet, as this example from golf course and driving range manager Playgolf illustrates:

> At the request of the company, trading on AIM for the under-mentioned securities has been temporarily suspended from 27/04/2009 1:30pm pending clarification of the company's financial position.

The phrase 'pending clarification of the company's financial position' is to be dreaded. Occasionally, although rarely, it really does mean that finances are being sorted out satisfactorily. In the overwhelming majority of cases the company is perfectly clear about its finances: they are in a mess.

This phrase means that the company is discussing with its banks whether the plug is about to be pulled or whether a big enough overdraft will be provided to allow the company to keep going. More often than not, plug pulling follows quite quickly.

Unfortunately it is now too late for shareholders to get out, as such a statement always means a suspension of share trading. The stock exchange would not allow share trading to continue until the position is clarified.

When you see this type of statement, assume that your shareholding is now worthless. If by any miracle the company returns from the living dead, count it as a bonus.

8.

Takeover Approaches

The most exciting time in stock market investing is to become embroiled in a takeover bid, either because you hold shares in a company on the receiving end of an offer (the target company) or because you are a shareholder in one making the offer (the bidder).

Apart from the announcement of a bid or a potential bid, there are two types of statement that will be issued as a matter of routine.

Firstly, the target company will state how many of its shares are in issue. The announcement will look like this one from Local Radio after a bid that we shall examine in more detail later in this chapter:

The Local Radio Company

Rule 2.10 Announcement

In accordance with Rule 2.10 of the City Code on Takeovers and Mergers, the Company confirms that it has 72,001,588 ordinary shares of 4p each in issue and admitted to trading on the AIM market of the London Stock Exchange under the ISIN code GB00B0108C60.

This is not of particular concern to the investor.

Secondly, there will usually be a welter of announcements by major shareholders recording any share sales or purchases they make in the target company. When a company is deemed to be 'in an offer period', which can mean that a potential as well as an actual bid is under consideration, shareholders with 1% or more must declare any share dealing in the interests of openness. This includes any deals made through derivatives such as contracts for difference as well as actual shares.

Such announcements will state the number of shares traded and at what price.

Keeping watch

While trading statements, company results and most other announcements are a one-day affair with a long gap to the next pronouncement, takeover situations should be monitored by shareholders day by day for any developments.

Similarly, routine statements invoke an instant decision on whether to buy or sell shares; takeovers involve serious reappraisals over a period of time, even when announcements are as bland as this one from clothing retailer Alexon:

Rejection of Approach

The Board of Alexon notes the recent rise in the Company's share price. The Board has received an unsolicited indication of interest from a third party to acquire the Company. No price or other terms were indicated. The Board of Alexon has considered the approach and has decided to reject it.

The Board is confident in the strategy being implemented by the Company's new management team and believes that progressing with this strategy is the best way to enhance shareholder value.

Many approaches are quietly rejected out of hand and we never hear about them but occasionally the market gets wind of something and a movement in the share price forces disclosure, as in this case.

Most approaches are 'unsolicited', which means that they have been made entirely on the instigation of the bidder. Occasionally a company, usually one that is in financial trouble, will canvass for bidders but the target company will then be negotiating from a position of weakness. Unsolicited bids are generally preferable for shareholders in target companies because the potential bidder has to do the running. In either case, there is no guarantee that a firm offer will be forthcoming.

Unsolicited bids are often rejected by the target company's directors as 'opportunistic'. This is a particularly meaningless epithet. All takeover approaches are made because the potential bidder sees an opportunity.

The Alexon board is perfectly entitled to reject the approach without putting it to shareholders. The unnamed suitor still has the right, if it so wishes, to appeal directly to Alexon shareholders by tabling a formal bid.

Alexon quite rightly states its reasons for rejecting the approach: no bid price has been mentioned and it has a new board with a new strategy. Its shareholders are similarly entitled to form their own opinions. They should consider whether they feel that the board and its strategy are going in the right direction.

Alexon is, for the time being 'in play' even though the approach has been rejected. Shareholders should be alert to the possibility of an offer emerging. They can also monitor any movements in the share price for an opportunity to sell in the market at a profit if they feel they want to get out.

Figure 8.1: Alexon

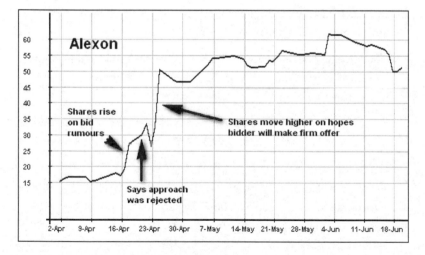

Alexon shares had collapsed from 250p to 10p over a period of 18 months. They moved up from 17.5p to 30p in three trading days before the announcement of the approach and moved higher in the following two days despite the rejection of the approach, the subsequent unveiling of a pre-tax loss and the absence of a dividend.

Choosing whether to stay in or get out

Not all takeover approaches are successful by any means. Indeed, many do not even reach the point of a firm offer. Shareholders in a target company need to read the company's statements to assess whether they should stay in for the ride or take advantage of any surge in the share price.

This is not always an easy choice, so it is all the more reason to be fully appraised of the situation.

One approach that came to nothing was at oil and gas explorer Bowleven, which correctly alerted the markets when, after months of going nowhere, its shares suddenly jumped from 34p to 41p in a single day's trading:

Statement re possible offer

Bowleven confirms that it has received a possible cash offer for the entire issued share capital of the Company at a price of 150 pence per ordinary share. The Board confirms that it would currently be minded to give its recommendation should a firm offer be made at such a price by the potential offeror.

The possible offer is subject to customary pre-conditions, including satisfactory completion of due diligence and final board approval of the potential offeror.

As required by the Takeover Code, Bowleven confirms that this announcement is being made without the agreement of the potential offeror.

For the avoidance of doubt, there can be no certainty that any offer will ultimately be made for the Company or as to the terms on which any such offer might be made, even if the pre-conditions are satisfied or waived.

A further announcement will be made when appropriate.

Don't think you have necessarily missed something when you see the word 'confirmed'. Companies are curiously fond of 'confirming' matters that have not been mentioned previously. Anyway, let's not quibble. This is undoubtedly good news.

Bowleven shares had slumped, along with the crude oil price, from 400p to 30p in the space of six months and were trading around 35p when this statement came out. Not surprisingly they shot up to 110p over the next two days.

Figure 8.2: Bowleven

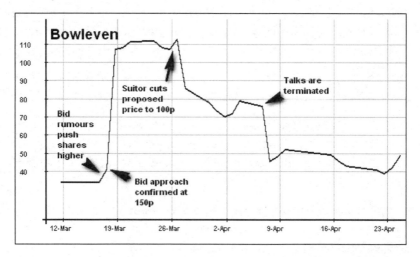

Pre-conditions

However, there was reason to be cautious and Bowleven shareholders did well to consider taking the profit that was available rather than hang on in the hope of an extra 40p.

Even the headline carried a warning: this is a possible, not a definite offer. And is this too good to be true? With a price tag more than quadruple the previous prevailing stock market price, you can bet that the board is more than 'minded to accept'. It will leap at such an offer.

It is not a particular worry that the offer is subject to 'customary preconditions'. These are conditions that the potential bidder, the *offeror* in takeover jargon, wishes to be met before a formal offer is actually launched.

It is quite normal for approaches to be made on this understanding. The would-be bidder does not yet have detailed knowledge of the operations of the target company and will want a look at the books before making a commitment.

Other possible pre-conditions include putting together the necessary finance, which is slightly ominous in that one would naturally prefer a would-be bidder to have already got the cash to pay for the bid. A common pre-condition is for the target company's directors to agree to recommend acceptance of the bid and to agree to accept for any shares that they own.

Shareholders are rarely told precisely what the pre-conditions are. Such approaches are often spurned, whereupon the bidder is likely to walk away.

In this case the bidder's board will have to meet again after seeing Bowleven's books to decide whether to proceed. This carrries the unfortunate implication that the bidder's board is not fully committed to the bid.

Under takeover rules, target companies must state whether any announcement is unilateral or whether it has been run past the potential bidder. Potential bidders generally prefer not to have news of the approach broadcast until there is a clear chance of success. Target companies are often obliged to make the approach known to prevent speculation in its shares.

This time we have no knowledge of who the bidder is, making it harder to judge the merits of the approach. If the announcement is made jointly then the other party will be named.

Lack of certainty

Bowleven quite rightly stresses that there is no certainty that a bid will be forthcoming. Even if there is a bid, it may be at a lower price. However, you would expect such wording on a statement of this kind to be added as routine.

The uncertainties of this kind of situation were brought home rather brutally just over a week later:

Update on possible cash offer

The board of Bowleven has received a revised possible offer from the potential offeror of 100 pence per ordinary share. The revised possible offer is not subject to due diligence and has received the necessary approval from the offeror's board of directors, but is subject to other customary pre-conditions.

The board of directors of Bowleven is not aware of any reason, whether arising from the due diligence or otherwise, that would explain the difference between the offer price approved by the potential offeror's board and the indicative offer price contained in the original approach.

The board of directors of Bowleven is currently considering the possible offer in consultation with certain major shareholders and a further update will be provided in due course.

This announcement has not been made with the agreement or approval of the potential offeror and there can be no certainty an offer will be made or as to the terms of any offer.

This really is very shabby, although one must stress that no blame attaches to the Bowleven board, which appears to have acted quite properly in exploring the approach. Shareholders who bought at 110p in the reasonable hope of a 40p profit have been sadly disillusioned.

Unfortunately when a bidder tries to renege on an indicated bid it carries an implication that it has discovered something nasty. In this case the unknown suitor is still talking about 100p a share and this time it has got past the suitor's board but the proposal is still not a firm bid.

The shares quickly fell back to 70p, reflecting the continued uncertainty over whether there would be an offer.

Although conditions still apply, the 100p is not conditional on due diligence. Presumably the suitor has seen the books in the meantime but has not indicated to Bowleven what is wrong. Is there a genuine problem or is this a bargaining ploy?

Talks are terminated

Alas, we shall probably never know as Bowleven decided enough was enough a few days later:

End of offer period

Discussions have now terminated and Bowleven is no longer in discussions with any party regarding a potential offer for the Company. As such, following consultation with the Panel on Takeovers and Mergers, the company is no longer in an offer period.

The board continues to believe that, despite the challenging market conditions, the outlook for the business remains extremely positive. In the last six months, the group has made significant progress in enhancing the value of its portfolio.

The immediate priority for the business is the drilling of an appraisal well on the IF oil discovery.

Bowleven continues to review all available funding options to progress the business and increase shareholder value. These include the potential farmout of part of the group's existing positions in Cameroon and Gabon and the raising of equity and debt finance. The group remains fully funded for its committed work programme during 2009.

While companies are the subject of a bid or a possible bid, even at the stage of preliminary talks, and this information is in the public arena, the target company is in what is known as an offer period. This means that all shareholders with more than 1% of the company's shares must declare any sales or purchases so that other shareholders have a fair idea of who is building stakes.

With the ending of the talks, Bowleven is no longer in an offer period. The company has attempted to calm nerves by stressing its positive view of the outlook and by making clear what actions it is taking to secure the future of the business.

Nonetheless, the shares slumped 30.5p to 42.5p on the day the talks collapsed.

When an offer is welcomed

An alternative scenario is that a bid is forthcoming and it is welcomed by the target company's board. Such a case is that of computer games publisher Eidos, which began thus:

Statement re Possible Offer

The Board of Eidos notes today's share price rise.

The Board can announce that it has received a preliminary approach which may or may not lead to an offer being made for the Company. Eidos emphasises that discussions are at a very early stage and that there can be no assurance that an offer will be forthcoming.

Further statements will be issued in due course as appropriate.

It came as some relief that shareholders might be put out of their misery after a series of setbacks and disappointments had sent the shares plummeting from 400p to 50p in the second half of 2007, followed by a further drifting to single figures in January 2009.

Bid rumours sparked a jump from 9p to 14p.

If talks are at such an early stage when news leaks out, shareholders often have to be patient while negotiations continue behind the scenes but in this case it was only a couple of weeks before a subsidiary of Square Enix, a Tokyo based supplier of software for games consoles, named its price:

The SQEX Directors and the Eidos Directors are pleased to announce that they have reached agreement on the terms of a recommended Offer under which SQEX, a wholly-owned subsidiary of Square Enix, will acquire the entire issued and to be issued ordinary share capital of Eidos. The Offer is to be effected by means of a scheme of arrangement.

Under the terms of the Offer, Eidos Shareholders will be entitled to receive 32 pence in cash for each Eidos Share held.

The Offer values the entire existing issued share capital of Eidos at approximately £84.3 million.

The Offer represents:

- a premium of approximately 258 per cent to the closing mid-market price of Eidos Shares on the London Stock Exchange of 9 pence per Eidos Share on 14 January 2009 (being the last Business Day prior to Eidos' announcement that it had received an approach that might or might not lead to an offer);

- a premium of approximately 129 per cent to the closing mid-market price of Eidos Shares on the London Stock Exchange of 14 pence per Eidos Share on 11 February 2009 (being the last practicable day prior to the date of this announcement);

- The Eidos Directors, who have been so advised by Citi, consider the terms of the Offer to be fair and reasonable. In providing its advice to the Eidos Directors, Citi has taken into account the commercial assessments of the Eidos Directors.

- The Eidos Directors intend unanimously to recommend that Eidos Shareholders vote in favour of the Scheme as those of them who are Shareholders have irrevocably undertaken to do in respect of their own beneficial holdings of 204,153 Eidos Shares in aggregate representing approximately 0.08 per cent of the existing issued share capital of Eidos.

- Insight Investment Management and Cazenove Capital Management Ltd. have irrevocably undertaken to vote in favour of the Scheme in respect of their aggregate holdings of 34,225,256 Eidos Shares representing approximately 13 per cent of the existing issued share capital of Eidos.

- Warner Bros Entertainment Inc. is contractually obliged under a Subscription Agreement with Eidos to provide an irrevocable undertaking in respect of 52,518,080 Eidos Shares representing approximately 20 per cent of the existing issued share capital of Eidos.

Formal offers always indicate the price being paid for the entire company but what matters to Eidos shareholders is how much per share they will get. The 32p on offer is three and a half times the level the shares had sunk to before the approach (a 258% premium means 9p plus an additional 258% or 23p on top) and more than double the 14p that the shares had reached before terms were announced (a 129% premium). The larger the premium, the greater the gain.

The proposed takeover is by a scheme of arrangement under which Eidos shareholders vote for or against it at an EGM. There is always the added safeguard that High Court approval is required for a scheme of arrangement so that shareholders are not unfairly bulldozed into accepting a bid.

Advice to shareholders

As is normal, the Eidos directors give advice to shareholders, in this case to vote in favour as they have consulted advisers and, in the time-honoured phrase, feel the terms are 'fair and reasonable'. However, this is only a recommendation. The shareholders own the company and they are each entitled to vote as they wish, with the proviso that under a scheme of arrangement a 75% vote in favour is binding on all shareholders.

Shareholders can see how the wind is blowing from the list of major shareholders who have committed themselves to voting in favour. Although the directors themselves have less than one tenth of a percent of the shares (hardly a vote of confidence in the company they are charged with running) a total of 33% is irrevocably committed, that is these shares will be voted in favour whatever happens in the meantime.

Key dates

Eidos shareholders soon received notification of the date and venue of the EGM, the date of the High Court hearing and, assuming the scheme was approved, other dates such as when Eidos shares would be de-listed from the stock exchange and when cheques would be posted.

You know it is all over when you see an announcement that says this:

> Eidos and SQEX are pleased to announce that, at the Court Meeting held earlier today, the Scheme was approved by the requisite majority.

Contested bids

If you are lucky, more than one definite bidder will emerge for a company where you hold shares. Such an event tends to happen at times of economic prosperity and rising share prices, where companies seem much more attractive.

UKRD and Hallwood bids for The Local Radio Company

Contested bids were few and far between after stock markets around the world slumped in the credit crunch. So the attempted takeover of tiny local media outfit The Local Radio Company stood out among the debris. With the advertising revenue that it relied on in short supply, Local Radio shares stood at a measly 1p each when rival media group UKRD, itself the owner of six commercial radio services, saw the chance to expand at comparatively little cost:

Cash Offer by UKRD for The Local Radio Company

Offer Highlights:

The UKRD Board is pleased to announce the terms of a cash offer for the entire issued and to be issued share capital of Local Radio not already owned by UKRD.

The Offer will be made on the basis of 2 pence per Local Radio Share.

The Offer represents a premium of 100 per cent to the Closing Price of 1 pence per Local Radio Share on 26 March 2009, being the latest practicable date prior to the release of the Announcement.

UKRD owns 9,725,000 Local Radio Shares representing approximately 13.51 per cent of the existing issued ordinary share capital of Local Radio.

UKRD has received an irrevocable undertaking to accept the Offer in respect of 11,520,000 Local Radio Shares from Trevor Smallwood, Chairman of UKRD, representing approximately 16.00 per cent of the existing issued share capital of Local Radio.

> Commenting on the Offer, Trevor Smallwood, Chairman of UKRD, said: "We believe the Offer represents an attractive premium over recent trading levels and is in the best interests of Local Radio Shareholders as a whole. The combination of UKRD and Local Radio will result in a stronger player in the local radio sector throughout the UK and an expanded service offering to listeners. We strongly believe that the Offer is considerably more attractive than the open offer proposal announced by Local Radio on 6 March 2009, which is totally unacceptable and could potentially result in loss of control of Local Radio to two Local Radio Directors and heavy dilution for other Local Radio Shareholders."

There are two important points here for Local Radio shareholders. Firstly, the bid price, lowly though it may be, is double the prevailing stock market price. In fact, since 1p is the middle price between the stock market buying and selling prices, the offer is probably four times as much as you could get by selling in the market.

Secondly, UKRD is well on the way to winning as it already holds 13.51% of Local Radio shares and its chairman holds a further 16%, give a starting total of almost 30%.

The existing alternative

To judge the merits of the offer fully, we need to backtrack to the previously announced open offer proposal that Smallwood refers to. Badly strapped for cash, Local Radio had already struck a deal to sell its Jazz Radio station and now proposed to raise £1.5m through an open offer that would, in effect, hand control to its own chairman, Anthony Gumbiner, without him having to make a full bid.

Shareholders would have the right to buy 42 shares for every five already held, paying just a quarter of one penny for each new share. Since such a hefty issue was unlikely to be taken up by shareholders, Local Radio had arranged for the issue to be underwritten mainly by Gumbiner's company Hallwood. In other words, Hallwood would buy shares rejected by other shareholders.

Since Gumbiner already held 28.3% of Local Radio and was taking up his own entitlement, the underwriting agreement looked certain to take his holding above 30%, at which level he would normally be obliged to bid for the whole company.

However, a waiver had been obtained from the Takeover Panel so he would not have to launch a bid. That was because Local Radio was on the verge of going bust, leaving shareholders with worthless shares.

UKRD's offer of 2p a share is clearly a much more attractive proposal.

Local Radio's response

However, Local Radio's response was low-key:

> The Board will consider the offer document once it is posted by UKRD and will respond to the Offer in due course.
>
> At this time the Board advises Local Radio's shareholders to take no action regarding the Offer until they have had the opportunity to consider the Board's response to the Offer.

This is perfectly reasonable and normal. Unless you want to take the opportunity of any rise in the share price to get out by selling in the market, there is no need to rush when a takeover is launched. In particular, you may regret accepting an offer in haste if a better offer comes along.

Do not be bullied into accepting an offer by phrases such as this:

> The UKRD Board strongly urges Local Radio Shareholders to accept the Offer without delay to hasten the availability of much needed funding from UKRD to Local Radio to enable it to continue trading.

The merits of patience

At that stage there were still two weeks to go before UKRD's offer was due to close and indeed, in the meantime Hallwood, the company associated with Local Radio's chairman, came up with a better deal:

> Hallwood is pleased to announce the terms of a cash offer for the entire issued and to be issued ordinary share capital of Local Radio not already owned by Hallwood.
>
> The Offer will be made on the basis of 2.5 pence in cash per Local Radio Share, valuing the entire issued share capital of Local Radio at approximately £1,800,040.
>
> The Offer is conditional upon Hallwood receiving minimum acceptances from not less than 90 per cent in nominal value of the Local Radio Shares. However, Hallwood reserves the right to elect to reduce this condition to such lesser percentage as Hallwood may elect (provided it has acquired more than 50% of the voting rights).
>
> If the Offer is declared unconditional in all respects then, provided Hallwood is not entitled to acquire compulsorily all remaining shares in TLR, Hallwood intends to maintain the admission to trading on AIM of the TLR Shares.

Hallwood has put a condition of 90% acceptances on its offer but it drops a strong hint that this requirement will be lowered to 50% in due course. Bidders often stipulate a 90% acceptance level at the outset because they know they can lower the threshold if they wish. Under the Takeover Code conditions may be waived but they cannot be increased once the bid has been launched.

It is the role of independent directors of the target company – that is, those who are not connected with any bid – to advise shareholders what action to take. In this case there was only one director who did not have some connection with either bidder and in due course he offered this comment:

> The independent non-executive director of The Local Radio Company plc announces his response to the Offer from UKRD Group Limited. The independent non-executive director has carefully considered all material aspects of the UKRD Offer and strongly recommends shareholders reject the UKRD Offer.

It's a bit wordy but you get the drift. Given that there is a higher offer on the table it would have been difficult to recommend this lower offer. Nonetheless, shareholders must make up their own minds. This is advice, not an order.

First closing date

A week later, the UKRD offer reached its first closing date and we can see that some Local Radio shareholders did accept:

> UKRD hereby notifies Local Radio Shareholders that as at 1pm on 21 April 2009, being the First Closing Date of the Offer, it has received valid acceptances of the Offer in respect of 16,761,083 Local Radio Shares, representing 23.27 per cent.
>
> Such acceptances include 11,520,000 Local Radio Shares, representing approximately 16 per cent, which were the subject of an irrevocable undertaking from Trevor Smallwood.
>
> Accordingly, UKRD now holds valid acceptances in respect of and has an interest in 26,486,083 Local Radio Shares in aggregate, representing approximately 36.78 per cent of Local Radio.
>
> Invesco Asset Management, acting for and on behalf of its discretionary managed clients, confirmed in a letter of intent that it is its intention to accept in respect of 3,914,416 Local Radio Shares, representing approximately 5.44 per cent of Local Radio. From the information available, UKRD believes that Invesco has accepted in respect of 830,584 Local Radio Shares, 1.15 per cent. Such shares have been included in the number of valid acceptances.
>
> The Offer is extended for a further 14 days and will remain open for acceptance until 1pm on 5 May 2009.

Pause for thought

Time to reflect and to pat ourselves on the back for not rushing into a decision, unlike some shareholders who presumably accepted this inferior offer prematurely before the better one came along. If more Local Radio shareholders had rushed in, UKRD might well have got past 50% and been able to declare its offer unconditional, thus freezing out the alternative offer.

Of the 23% acceptances, 16% is from the chairman of the bidder. Fund manager Invesco is playing a curious game, apparently committing its clients to the UKRD bid but actually accepting for only 1.15% out of the

5.44% it manages. Stripping out these two supporters from the 23.27% indicates that 6.12% of other shareholders accepted. This is quite a high level for a first closing date, especially when there is an alternative bid. In such cases acceptances usually tot up to less then 1%.

UKRD now owns or has acceptances for 36.78% of Local Radio shares, a good step on the way to 50% but still well short. With 14 days to go to the second closing date there is still time to await developments.

Meanwhile the shares were trading at 2.5p. Even allowing for the spread between the buying and selling price it was possible to sell in the market for 2p a share and get your money now, so why accept the UKRD offer and have to wait?

The bidder

So far we have looked at announcements from the perspective of shareholders in the target company but you are just as likely to have invested in the bidder. Here the benefits are less clear-cut and will in any case come through some time in the future.

BG Group bids for Pure Energy Resources

Energy company BG became embroiled in a bidding war for Australian company Pure Energy Resources, which produces methane gas from coal seams.

BG emerged as a natural gas producer from the break-up of British Gas, with the retail side forming Centrica as an entirely separate company. BG has been ambitious, with international aspirations, and it had recently bought the Queensland Gas Company in an agreed bid costing £2 billion.

Usually companies prefer to digest one acquisition before embarking on the next but BG was prompted into further action when Arrow Energy, a producer of coal seam gas in eastern Australia and Asia, launched a A$673m takeover bid for Pure Energy (about £330 million at the prevailing exchange rate).

The offer was part cash and part Arrow shares and valued Pure shares at A\$5.40 each. Note that the value of an offer wholly or partly in shares will vary according to changes in the bidder's share price.

The bid battle starts

Pure would fit in with BG's existing, expanded operations in Australia but BG was caught on the hop and, not unreasonably, it took seven weeks to put together a counterbid:

BG Group makes A\$796 million takeover offer for Pure

BG today announced its intention to make an all-cash takeover offer to acquire all of the issued shares in Pure Energy Resources for A\$6.40 per share.

BG's Offer represents:

- a 19% premium to the implied value of the Arrow Offer of A\$5.39 per share; and

- a 115% premium to Pure's closing share price of A\$2.98 on 19 December 2008, being the last full day of trading before the Arrow Offer was announced.

BG's Offer gives Pure shareholders the certainty of cash at a time of heightened uncertainty in world equity and financial markets.

BG has acquired a relevant interest in approximately 10% of Pure shares from a range of shareholders. The Arrow Offer is subject to a 90% minimum acceptance condition. BG does not intend to accept the Arrow offer because it does not intend to own Arrow shares.

BG's offer is subject to:

- a minimum acceptance condition of 50.1%;
- Foreign Investment Review Board (FIRB) approval

The most important point is how valuations tend to leap when more than one bidder is interested in a company. Pure shares were trading on the Australian stock market at only A$2.98 before Arrow's bid. BG is offering more than twice as much – an additional 115% (referred to in the announcement as the premium).

In order to scare off Arrow from competing, BG has pitched its offer 19% higher, almost one fifth extra. The Arrow share price has eased very slightly so that its offer is now worth one Australian cent less than when it was announced.

Another advantage of the BG offer from the point of view of Pure shareholders is that it is all in cash, while accepting the Arrow offer means that they will be lumbered with Arrow shares that they may not want.

Conditional bids

Bids normally have conditions attached. These may involve raising finance or receiving the backing of the target company's board. They will always be conditional on gaining a minimum level of acceptances.

The more conditions that have to be fulfilled, the greater the odds against the bid succeeding. If you own shares in the target company it can be worth accepting a lower bid that is conditional only on a minimum level of acceptances rather than stick out for a higher one that still has to meet other conditions.

The BG bid will go unconditional if shareholders with 50.1% of the shares accept. In other words, BG will settle for the minimum level of ownership that gives full control and will be content if necessary to accommodate a large minority of Pure shareholders rejecting its offer.

The 10% of shares that existing Pure shareholders have committed to BG will count towards the 50.1%, so BG is already well on the way. Acquiring a relevant interest means BG does not yet actually own the shares but it is in the process of buying them from the existing shareholders.

That 10% is important in another way. Since the Arrow bid is conditional on 90% acceptances and BG does not intend to accept, the Arrow bid is effectively blocked by BG's 10%. It is quite common for bids to be initially conditional on such a high level of acceptances because in Australia, as in the UK, a successful bidder can force all shareholders in the target company to accept once it gets over 90%.

There is, however, nothing to stop Arrow from dropping the threshold to 50.1% if it wishes.

Assessing rival merits

Naturally bidders tend to stress the merits of their own offer. If you hold shares in a target company you should always read all statements from all sides as perceived benefits may be disputed.

In this case the superiority of the BG case is clear-cut – higher price, all cash and lower acceptance level required – except for one possible stumbling block: the approval of the Australian Foreign Investment Review Board.

It is quite normal for bids, wherever in the world they are made, to depend on approval from the relevant regulatory authority or authorities, possibly in more than one country. In this case the Foreign Investment Review Board studies all bids that involve foreign companies buying Australian resource companies.

Arrow quickly raised its offer to A\$3 cash plus 1.57 Arrow shares, valuing Pure shares at A\$7.18 each, so BG put out a holding statement:

BG Group takeover offer for Pure – Update

BG is considering its position and will advise the market of its decision.

BG recommends that shareholders and directors of Pure take no action in relation to the Arrow offer before then.

It is quite common in takeovers for one party or another to urge shareholders to take no action but shareholders should always consider whether sitting tight is their best option. Remember, the board of the target company or any bidder may have a vested interest in maintaining the status quo. Shareholders are likewise entitled to do what is in their own best interest.

In this case, it is usually right for shareholders in the target company to hold on during a bidding war, especially where at least one firm offer has been made. The worst that can happen is that you have to settle for the existing bid while the potential gain from one or more higher bids is very attractive.

Matters come to a head

BG did not waste much time pondering and came back very quickly with:

Pure recommends BG Group takeover offer

BG Group cash offer now A$8.00 per share

BG Group offer values Pure at A$995 million

BG Group will pay accepting Pure shareholders within 5 business days of the receipt by BG Group of their acceptance

Unanimous recommendation by Pure's independent directors, subject to there being no superior proposal

Pure's independent directors, who together have an interest in approximately 12% of Pure, intend to accept the increased BG Group offer within 7 days, subject to there being no superior proposal

Key shareholders, Tom Fontaine and Karl Meade (who have an interest in approximately 5% and 3%, respectively, of Pure), intend to accept the increased BG Group offer within 7 days, subject to there being no superior proposal

BG Group's increased offer represents:

- a 168% premium to Pure's closing share price of A$2.98 on 19 December 2008, being the last full day of trading before the Arrow offer was first announced; and

- an 11% premium to the implied value of the Arrow offer of A$7.181 on 18 February 2009.

BG Group's revised offer is unconditional.

It seems as if BG has already won: it has the unanimous support of the independent directors (those who will not be staying on at the company after the takeover so have no personal gain from backing BG) with 12%; it has the backing of two major shareholders with 8% between them; it is offering a higher price than the only other bidder; and it is no longer attaching any conditions to its offer, which usually happens only when victory is in the bag (remember, one condition of all bids is gaining overall control with at least 50.1% of the shares).

However, those acceptances can be switched if Arrow comes back with a more attractive offer. In any case, BG is not claiming it has 50% of Pure shares. It said earlier that it could count on 10% of Pure shares and now has the commitment of a further 20% so it is apparently prepared to settle for 30% if push comes to shove.

This perceived victory is at quite a price. BG is now offering more than two and a half times the level of the Pure share price before the bidding war started and 11% more than the increased offer from Arrow.

Paying more to be sure

But BG was not finished yet:

> BG Group final offer for Pure at $8.25, subject to acquiring 90% interest.
>
> BG will increase its recommended all-cash takeover offer for Pure Energy Resources from A$8.00 to A$8.25 per share, on condition that BG has acquired a relevant interest in 90% of Pure's ordinary share capital by the close of the BG Group offer period.
>
> The conditional offer price of $8.25 is final in the absence of a superior proposal.
>
> The independent directors of Pure, together with key shareholders Tom Fontaine and Karl Meade, have now accepted the BG Offer.
>
> BG Group is now the largest shareholder in Pure, with a relevant interest in 28.9% of Pure's ordinary share capital.

BG is prepared to pay another 25 Australian cents on top of its A$8 offer if it gets acceptances for more than 90%. Having the right to buy out the minority shareholders is worth paying for because it removes the administrative costs of keeping separate accounts and mailing them to a rump of Pure shareholders.

Even now, BG is keeping open the option of coming back with an even higher offer if it is outbid by Arrow or anyone else; otherwise the offer is final, which means it will not be changed in any way.

The battle ends

In the event, Arrow decided enough was enough and allowed its offer to lapse, leaving BG as the only bidder. By now BG had 36% of Pure and Royal Dutch Shell, with 11%, accepted the bid, giving 47%. Within days the tally was up to 70%, giving majority control.

Then came:

BG Group acquires relevant interest in more than 90% of Pure

BG has now acquired a relevant interest in 90.93% of the ordinary share capital of Pure Energy Resources under its recommended all cash takeover Offer for Pure.

Its offer price will be increased from A$8.00 to A$8.25 per Pure share.

And finally:

BG Group will now proceed to compulsory acquisition of all the remaining Pure shares

Pure shareholders who validly accept BG Group's Offer will have their payment of A$8.25 per share despatched within 5 business days of the receipt by BG Group of a valid acceptance.

Pure shareholders who do not accept BG Group's Offer before it closes will have their shares compulsorily acquired. In accordance with time periods specified under the Corporations Act, compulsory acquisition will involve a delay in payment to Pure shareholders of approximately six weeks.

Shareholders, especially long standing ones who feel some loyalty to their company, sometimes resent having to accept a bid but there really is no point in refusing to accept the inevitable.

Other shareholders bury their heads in the sand, failing to read the documents sent to them and thus missing out on opportunities.

The laggards now have a choice: accept the offer and be paid within five days or do nothing and wait six weeks for the cash. The sensible choice is obvious.

What is not obvious, until months or years hence, is whether BG has overpaid for Pure and whether it will be able to recoup the outlay in increased profits.

Mergers

Sometimes two companies come together through a merger rather than by one taking over the other. Rather confusingly, takeovers are sometimes dressed up as mergers either as a face-saving exercise for the directors of the target company or as an attempt to hide the absence of a bid premium.

In a genuine merger two companies come together on an equal footing. Usually a new holding company will be set up and shareholders in the two merging companies will be given shares in the new company in place of their old ones.

How many shares you get will depend on the respective sizes of the merging companies. Although technically a merger is a joining of equals, the allocation of shares will usually depend on the relative sizes of the partners.

Thus when the two commercial television franchisees Granada and Carlton came together to form ITV, more shares were allocated to Granada shareholders because it was the larger partner.

The simplest way of dividing the spoils is to take the stock market capitalisations of the two companies immediately before the proposed merger is announced.

Other factors such as the assets of the partners may cause an adjustment to the ratio. Mergers can be less straightforward than takeovers because it is not always clear whether one set of shareholders is getting more out of the deal than the other.

In theory, everyone gains because they now hold shares in a stronger company. However, if the stock market believes that one partner is getting more out of the deal than the other then the share prices may move in different directions, changing the market capitalisations. In that case the boards of the merging companies will have to decide whether to base the deal on the previous share price or the new one.

It is likely that the chairman of the new company will come from one side of the merger and the chief executive from the other with the rest of the board positions similarly split. Again, that is what happened with Granada and Carlton.

Case study: Peter Hambro/Aricom

The merger of mining companies Peter Hambro and Aricom actually began as a proposed takeover as the first announcement indicated:

> Peter Hambro Mining confirms that it is in preliminary discussions with Aricom regarding a possible offer by Peter Hambro Mining for the entire issued share capital of Aricom. The consideration for any such offer would comprise shares in Peter Hambro Mining. The discussions are at a very preliminary stage and there is no certainty that any offer will be made or, if such an offer is forthcoming, the terms of such offer.

This soon changed as talks progressed:

> The Independent Board Committees of Peter Hambro Mining and Aricom have made considerable progress towards reaching agreement on the terms of a recommended Merger of the two companies by which all of the issued share capital of Aricom would be acquired by Peter Hambro Mining. The Independent Board Committees are hopeful that final agreement will be reached shortly.

Agreement has not yet been reached on the exchange ratio for the Merger and certain other terms and there can therefore be no certainty that the Merger will proceed.

However, the Independent Board Committees are working towards agreement on a fixed exchange ratio which would result in Aricom Shareholders receiving one fully paid Peter Hambro Mining Share in exchange for between 15.77 and 17.14 fully paid Aricom Shares. The fixed exchange ratio (which would be in this range) is expected to be based on a number of factors which are still subject to negotiation between the parties.

Peter Hambro Mining is also today launching a Placing to raise approximately £55 million. The Placing proceeds are expected to increase working capital headroom for Peter Hambro Mining, and, should the Merger proceed, the Enlarged Group.

What makes this a merger?

Although Aricom shareholders will receive Hambro shares, this is not a takeover as such, although the lines are a little blurred. Over the next few weeks Hambro itself sometimes called the planned deal a merger and at other times an acquisition.

In a bid, one side sets the terms for buying the other party. While the two sides may discuss the terms in the hope of agreeing a deal, in the end the bidder decides the price and will usually agree to pay a premium on top of the stock market price of the target company.

In this case the ratio of shares is being worked out mutually on the basis of how much the two sides are contributing to the enlarged group rather than Hambro setting the price it feels it is prepared to offer for Aricom.

There is clearly still some way to go in settling the exact ratio. As yet we have only a quite wide target range.

The waters are further muddied by a share placing that Hambro is simultaneously carrying out. These new shares will have to be taken into account in setting the ratio.

A deal was soon struck:

Recommended Merger of Peter Hambro Mining and Aricom

Under the terms of the Merger:

Aricom Shareholders will receive one fully paid New Peter Hambro Mining Share in exchange for 16 fully paid Aricom Shares; and

Existing Peter Hambro Mining Shareholders will hold 47.4 per cent of the Enlarged Group;

Aricom Shareholders will hold 43.2 per cent of the Enlarged Group;

the Placees will hold 9.4 per cent of the Enlarged Group;

Peter Hambro Mining intends to make an application to obtain a primary listing on the Official List as soon as possible.

The Enlarged Group will be led by a team comprising Peter Hambro as Executive Chairman, Pavel Maslovskiy as CEO and Brian Egan as CFO and the non-executive directors are expected to be Sir Rudolph Agnew, Sir Malcolm Field, Lord Guthrie, Peter Hill-Wood and Sir Roderic Lyne.

So, the merged entity retains the name and stock market quotation of Peter Hambro and the merger is carried out as if Hambro is taking over Aricom. We can see that Hambro shareholders get a slightly larger share of the cake than Aricom and those shareholders stumping up cash in the placing also receive a slice.

Hambro supplies the executive chairman and the chief executive while the chief financial officer comes from Aricom. Hambro provides three non-executives and Aricom two, reflecting the larger size of Hambro. Despite this being a merger, it is clear that Hambro is the dominant partner.

Investors decided that the enlarged group was indeed stronger than the separate parts with a strong balance sheet after the placing and a move up from AIM to the main market.

Joint ventures

Joint ventures, where two unconnected companies come together to cooperate in running an operation, are a kind of halfway house between going it alone and a full-scale merger.

The two parties may establish a joint venture (JV) to bring together two existing subsidiaries, one from each partner, or as an entirely new operation that gives the partners access to a new market or a new geographic area.

These are tricky arrangements and shareholders need to look carefully at how the JV is structured and the thinking behind it to judge the potential benefits for either side.

Most JVs are formed on a 50:50 basis but one side may have a majority stake. Where there are more than two partners, the stakes will be split into smaller but not necessarily equal slices.

The advantages are that both sides bring something to the party and JVs tend to work best when each side puts in different expertise or assets. Thus one partner may contribute cash or property while the other has the skills to run the business.

Partners may split the cost of setting up the JV and also the running costs when the total would be beyond the resources of either acting separately. They share the risk of failure and they share any profits.

Points of contention

On the other hand, who is to run the business?

In a 50-50 JV both sides have an equal say so unless the two parties agree, nothing gets done. If one party has a majority stake, then the junior party may become gradually disenchanted with the arrangement, especially if the JV is less successful than expected.

Where the two sides are putting in assets, it is possible for an independent expert to put a value on those assets. Where a company is putting in expertise there is no tangible value so it is hard to assess whether both partners are making an equal contribution.

While JVs tend to be between two partners, because it is easier to reach agreement on costs and strategy the fewer partners there are, there is no reason why several partners cannot come together.

The more partners there are, the more the costs are divided, although the potential rewards will also be divided into smaller parcels. One advantage of having several partners is that voting rights can be split so that, unless one partner has a 50% stake, it is always possible to resolve any disagreement through a majority vote.

One other possible point of contention is when the JV is renting property or buying supplies from one or both of the partners. Who decides on prices paid? Who decides which of the partners supplies the goods?

It is therefore not surprising that many joint ventures, launched with good intent and a fanfare of trumpets, come to grief within very few years.

In assessing the potential of a JV, shareholders should consider why it is being set up. Will it expand the businesses of the partners, bringing them extra sales and profits, or are the partners struggling to cut costs in a shrinking market that will no longer support more than one supplier?

Case study: Stagecoach

Take this example from transport operator Stagecoach:

Sightseeing joint venture in New York

Stagecoach entered into an agreement to create a new joint venture to operate the sightseeing services of the Group's Gray Line New York business and the business of CitySights NY.

The Group's North American Division operates a successful sightseeing business in New York City, trading as Gray Line New York. Gray Line New York operates double decker bus, motorcoach and trolley bus tours of New York City and the surrounding area as well as other related services.

CitySights also operates sightseeing bus services in and around New York City.

The Group and CitySights NY will contribute vehicles, licences and certain other assets to the Joint Venture. In return, the Group will hold 50% of the voting rights and 60% of the economic rights in the Joint Venture with CitySights NY holding the remaining voting rights and economic rights. A Board of Directors, including representatives from both shareholders, will oversee the Joint Venture.

The Joint Venture will deliver a number of benefits:

- Customers will benefit from a good quality, high value, and better co-ordinated service with a range of products to choose from.

- A better co-ordinated service should reduce road congestion at certain points and enhance the value of the tours.

- The Joint Venture will benefit from cost savings and other synergies that arise from combining the two existing businesses to the extent permitted by existing contractual arrangements and other business considerations.

> The gross assets that the Group will contribute to the Joint Venture had a net book value of US$22.5m at 28 February 2009 and the gross assets that CitySights NY will contribute to the Joint Venture had a net book value of US$6.1m at 28 February 2009. For the year ended 30 April 2008, Gray Line New York contributed US$17.3m to the Group's operating profit. For the 12 months ended 31 January 2009, CitySights NY reported an operating profit of US$8.7m. More recent trading in the New York sightseeing market has been adversely affected by poor economic conditions and a weaker tourist market.

Despite the generally ebullient nature of the announcement, this is a setback. Reading between the lines we can see that the contraction in the number of tourists has made it uneconomic to run major bus tours of New York. Hence the two rivals are forced into what could be an uneasy pact.

Who gets what?

There will be some savings in fuel and staff in running fewer buses but the venture will now have surplus buses on its hands.

Stagecoach is putting more valuable assets into the joint venture than its rival CitySights, both in terms of the value of the buses and the profits that they make. Stagecoach assets are valued in the books at more than double those of CitySights while its profits are almost exactly double.

In consequence it will receive 60% of the profits of the JV, which seems to slightly favour CitySights. However, the valuations are historic so there may have been some adjustment for changes in values and profits over recent months.

Voting rights will be split 50-50, which certainly does favour CitySights. Day-to-day running will be in the hands of a separate board with representatives from both sides. They should manage to agree, as their interests in ensuring a success enterprise are identical – but you never know.

Will it last?

One sentence in the statement is worthy of comment:

> The new Joint Venture will operate services under both the Gray Line and CitySights brands and will be the leading provider of sightseeing bus services in New York.

So both brands will be retained. This saves the expense of repainting all the buses and altering the literature but is likely to cause some confusion among the travelling public who will think there are still two lines when there is really only one.

Perhaps the important point is that the two brands can be separated again if trade picks up. That will be a happier signal for Stagecoach shareholders than the forming of this joint venture.

Figure 8.3: Stagecoach

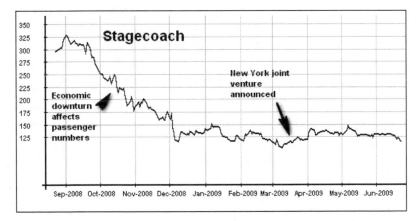

Stagecoach shares had plunged from over 300p to 101p in the six month before the joint venture was announced and investors decided that action to reduce costs was to be welcomed. Over the following two weeks the shares edged up to 125p.

9.
Rights Issues and Placings

Rights issues are a mixed blessing. If one is announced by a company in which you have invested, it is important to study the details carefully. Too many shareholders throw the bumph in the bin and bury their heads in the sand.

In fact, announcements of rights issues tend to be models of clarity. They state the following important points:

1. how many shares existing shareholders will be allowed to subscribe for

2. the price at which new shares are to be issued

3. the total amount of money that is being raised

4. the total number of new shares and the proportion that this will be of the enlarged issued share capital

5. why the rights issue is being made and how the cash raised will be used

Case study: Hammerson

A rights issue announcement by property group Hammerson began:

> Hammerson announces a fully underwritten Rights Issue to raise net proceeds of £584.2 million, which will be used to reduce drawn borrowings and net indebtedness. The Rights Issue is subject to approval by shareholders at a General Meeting to be held on 25 February 2009.

So immediately we have key facts: We know how much is being raised, that it will be used to reduce debt and that it is underwritten, so the issuing of new shares will go ahead even if existing shareholders spurn the opportunity to buy them because new investors are waiting in the wings to snap up any shares that are not taken.

We know that the issue cannot go ahead without the approval of shareholders (though this is usually a foregone conclusion as rights issues are rarely voted down) and that we have the opportunity to confront the board at a general meeting if we so wish.

The date of the meeting is potentially important because it is likely that the chairman will offer some update on trading and/or strategy to encourage a yes vote.

The important details

We then get some nitty gritty:

Highlights

- 7 for 5 fully underwritten Rights Issue of approximately 405.8 million New Shares at £1.50 per share to raise net proceeds of £584.2 million.

- The net proceeds will be used to reduce Hammerson's net indebtedness and substantially strengthen the Company's overall financial position.

- The Rights Issue will reduce pro forma gearing to 81% based on Hammerson's financial statements as at 31 December 2008.

The first point tells us how many shares we can subscribe for. Remember, shareholders are not obliged to take up all of their entitlement. They may opt for fewer shares or none at all.

In this case the rights issue is a hefty one. Shareholders are being asked to buy even more shares than they already own. If they take up their entitlement they will end up with 12 shares compared with five now.

The dilemma is whether taking up the rights issue will be throwing good money after bad. To stump up will be a burden but to refuse to do so will result in one's holding being diluted by new shareholders.

The decision is assisted by looking at the price at which the new shares will be issued. At 150p they were very much cheaper than the stock market value of existing shares, which had traded at 397p, more than double that amount, immediately before the rights issue was announced.

Even better, the shares rose 35.75p to 432.75p on the day of the announcement. Thus, for those who could scrape together the cash but did not want to hang onto the new shares, there was every hope of being able to sell the shares in the market at a profit subsequently.

What the rights issue is for

Less encouraging is the purpose of the rights issue. This is not to fund profitable expansion but to repair a large hole in the finances. As the announcement explained:

> Over the last eighteen months, the Board of Hammerson has taken measures to manage the Company's gearing, including selling assets and reducing development expenditure. It has also cut overheads. Since 30 June 2007, the Company has sold assets and used the net proceeds of £783 million to repay debt. The Company continues to pursue asset sales as a means of reducing gearing. However, given the lack of debt finance available to potential purchasers to fund acquisitions, negotiations regarding sales are proving protracted and the outcomes uncertain.
>
> In the event that the Company is unable to execute disposals and that the market value of the Group's property portfolio continues to decline, there is a risk that the Company could breach its gearing covenant in the future. The Board has therefore evaluated the option of seeking to renegotiate the Company's financial covenants both in its bank facilities and bonds. However, in current debt market conditions, any renegotiation would be difficult to achieve, particularly in relation to our bonds, and would also result in significantly increased financing costs.

So the company is in a bit of a bind. It must reduce its debts in order to reduce its gearing (which measures the level of its debts against the aggregate value of its assets). It is normal for property companies to have high levels of gearing but the banks have set a limit, referred to as the gearing covenant.

Unfortunately property prices have fallen and Hammerson's assets are now worth less. Debt as a percentage of the value of assets has thus risen to the point where the figure could go through the limit set by the banks.

It has gone as far as it can in selling assets, especially as potential buyers are having difficulty in the credit crunch raising cash to pay with. To sell more shopping centres or retail parks would mean parting with them at distressed prices and would reduce the value of assets owned even further. Yet a failure to raise cash carries the risk of Hammerson being penalised by the banks for breaking the gearing covenant.

Costs have already been cut as far as possible without sufficient impact. The rights issue is, in effect, a last resort.

A sop to shareholders

There is, however, an important sop to shareholders, and that concerns the dividend. After all, we want to know what we are likely to get out of the company if we are going to put more money in. Here is the good news:

> ### Dividends
>
> The Company is recommending a final dividend of 15.3 pence per share for 2008 (unchanged over 2007). This is subject to shareholder approval at the AGM to be held on 30 April 2009 and will be paid to shareholders on the register as at 20 February 2009.
>
> Accordingly the total dividend for the year will be 27.9 pence per share (compared with 27.3 pence for the year ended 31 December 2007), which represents dividend cover of 1.36 times. Applying the same dividend cover to pro forma 2008 adjusted earnings, restated for the effects of the Rights Issue, would result in a pro forma dividend for 2008 of 15.0 pence per share. This takes into account the new number of shares following the Rights Issue and the

> interest saving on the debt which will be repaid from the proceeds of the Rights Issue. The Board intends to maintain its policy of progressive dividend growth in the future from this base of 15.0 pence per share in respect of 2008.

The final dividend for the past year is to be maintained at the same level as the previous year. Note that this will be paid only on existing shares, not on any shares bought in the rights issue (which will not qualify for a dividend until the following financial year).

The interim dividend was actually raised slightly (hence the small increase in the total) but one could hardly expect a repeat of the final given the difficult financial circumstances. On the contrary, the increase in the interim, at a time when the storm clouds were already gathering, seems somewhat rash in hindsight.

Hammerson proposes that the total payout in the following financial year will be unchanged. However, the total will be divided among more than twice as many shares, so you would expect the dividend per share will be less than half.

This year's total is 27.9p so you would expect next year's total to be less than 14p. However, using the cash raised in the rights issue to reduce debt will chop a hefty slice off Hammerson's interest bill, and some of the saving will be added to the dividend, pushing the total up to 15p.

Case study: Cookson

The rights issue proposed by industrial materials group Cookson is an extreme case but one worth noting nonetheless as it sent conflicting signals to shareholders.

The company was hit particularly hard during the economic downturn, being heavily dependent on the steel industry and vehicle manufacturers, two sectors that saw production fall heavily. It also supplies products used to make iron and glass.

> **Cookson Group plc announces an underwritten Rights Issue to raise net proceeds of approximately £240 million**
>
> The Board of Cookson today announces a fully underwritten 12 for 1 Rights Issue to raise proceeds of approximately £240 million, net of expenses, through the issue of 2,551,293,144 New Shares. The Rights Issue has been fully underwritten by J.P. Morgan Securities and Merrill Lynch International.

Cookson gave two reasons for raising cash:

1. to provide a more suitable capital structure for the current environment; and

2. to enhance covenant and longer-term liquidity headroom under current debt facilities.

The two bullet points are a bit of company-speak. In the first one, Cookson is trying to say that it would be better to have less debt.

Beware of phrases such as 'suitable capital structure'. This sort of expression is trotted out to mean whatever is in fashion at the time. Until the credit crunch struck, companies were talking about running up debt as creating 'a more efficient balance sheet'!

The second bullet point is saying that if Cookson does not raise cash it is in danger of breaching the covenants on its loans. Expect companies to dress up unpleasant realities in fancy phrases.

What leaps out of the announcement is that shareholders are being invited to buy 12 new shares for each one already held. Usually shareholders are asked to buy fewer shares than they already hold. To be expected to multiply their holdings 12-fold is almost unheard of.

Cookson said it was dealing with an 'unprecedented downturn', which goes some way to explaining the unprecedented size of the rights issue. It was closing six factories in various countries and laying off 1,250 of its 17,000 workforce.

The total amount of money being raised, £240 million, is relevant. Cookson's statement makes clear that the cash will be used to reduce debts, currently standing at £732 million. So even after the rights issue, two thirds of the debt will remain a burden on the company.

Net proceeds is the amount of money the company will actually receive after deducting costs. In this case the rights issue is fully underwritten, in other words investment banks J.P.Morgan Securities and Merrill Lynch International will buy any new shares rejected by Cookson's existing shareholders, taking the whole lot if necessary.

An underwriting arrangement guarantees Cookson the cash but a fee will have to be paid to the underwriters in return for their guarantee. You can easily calculate the gross total being raised by multiplying the number of shares to be issued by the issue price. In this case 2,551,293,144 new shares at 10p each equals £255,129,314. So, that's over £15 million gone in expenses (since Cookson will receive £240 million net).

The trouble with rights issues is that they involve a lot of administration, which is why companies prefer to place shares with institutions.

Background to the issue

Unfortunately, because it is making such a massive rights issue, Cookson is obliged to offer the shares at a very cheap price to persuade investors to stump up the cash. The 10p issue price compares with a stock market price of 92p immediately before the capital raising was announced. The company provides the following background:

Background

- Cookson's profile has been transformed since 2003, through disposals, increased focus on higher technology products, cost reduction, and migration of manufacturing base to emerging markets.

- Acquisition of Foseco, financed by debt and equity, announced in October 2007 as next stage of Cookson's strategic development.

- Rapid and significant softening in Cookson's end-markets since late September 2008.

- Cookson expects a recovery in global steel production, to which over 40 per cent of Group trading profit is linked, later in 2009.

- Cookson benefits from attractive debt financing terms put in place at time of the Foseco acquisition, with, as at 31 December 2008, £794 million of committed bank facilities with remaining average maturity of 3.2 years.

Here we have the company putting a great gloss on things. Reading the background, one is entitled to wonder why the company needs such a massive rights issue if it is doing so well!

Apparently Cookson has been transformed and its debt is on attractive terms. As always when the statement seems to be at odds with the facts, look a little deeper.

Understanding the clues

The main clue is in the middle bullet point, placed where its impact is minimised: a sharp fall in sales has lasted for nearly six months. Recovery is not expected for another six months at least.

Human nature being what it is, companies in this position tend to underestimate the time that recovery will take. Such statements should be read in the context of the current world economic climate.

However attractive the terms, the Foseco acquisition is the cause of the debt pile. Clearly profits from the acquisition are not coming through, or not coming through quickly enough to pay off the borrowings.

Cookson says that this attractively financed debt is for an average 3.2 years, which implies there is no great rush to pay it off. However, quite apart from the danger of breaching banking covenants, which usually invokes a severe penalty and the end of attractive terms, an average implies that some debt will be due for repayment sooner.

Action taken

Cookson explains what it has been doing to get through the downturn:

Management response to market conditions

- Phase 1: Initiatives implemented since September 2008 to reduce employment costs with anticipated savings of £17 million per annum from early 2009.

- Phase 2: Six plant closures and further headcount reductions initiated last week, expected to result in savings of £23 million per annum from mid 2009.

- Total headcount reduction from both phases of approximately 1,250.

- Focus on cash generation measures and reduced levels of capital expenditure.

- Suspension of dividend payments until such time as Group's end-markets have recovered sufficiently.

It is encouraging that Cookson has taken action already but it has apparently not been enough. It is worth noting that the action began after the start of the downturn in markets and shareholders can reasonably ponder whether the company reacted too slowly to events that were well flagged earlier in the year.

Note also that reducing the number of employees always costs money immediately in the form of redundancy payments but the saving on wages take time to feed through. Likewise closing factories tends to take time to pay back initial costs.

Cookson is cutting back on spending, which we would expect given the state of its main markets. However, it is right to keep some investment going as it needs to be ready for the upturn when it comes.

Finally we get the killer punch as far as shareholders are concerned. The dividend is scrapped so there will be no final dividend for 2008 and, on current reckoning, no interim for 2009. The final dividend for 2009 must also be in doubt. The longer the downturn lasts, the more Cookson will need to conserve cash.

Profit projection

Cookson quite properly gave a projection of profit figures for 2008, although the final accounts had not yet been completed. These suggest a 34% increase in revenue and a 16% increase in profits.

Profit estimate for the year ended 31 December 2008

	2008	2007 As reported	Change
Revenue	Not less than £2,175m	£1,620m	34%
Trading profit	Not less than £213m	£170m	25%
Return on sales	Not less than 9.8%	10.5%	(0.7) pts
EBITDA	Not less than £260m	£204m	27%
Headline profit before tax	Not less than £174m	£150m	16%
Headline earnings per share	Not less than 58.0p	54.4p	7%
Net debt	Approximately £732m	£51m	Up £681m

The change in return on sales is shown in brackets as it is a negative figure. In other words, profit margins are down.

As we were into February at this stage, it was reasonable to assume that the figures could be viewed with a fair degree of certainty. Remember, though, that the figures would be inflated by the addition of Foseco. Note also that profits have risen more slowly than sales.

Figure 9.1: Cookson

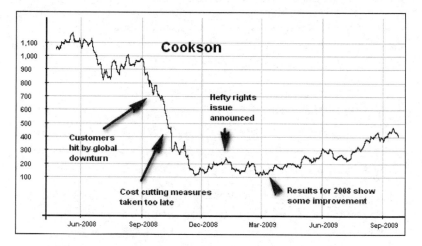

It was important for shareholders to read the statement and assess its implications quickly. Although Cookson shares initially lost almost half their value on the day after the rights issue was announced, they bounced back to close at a higher level than the previous night's close.

Investors who did not want to stump up more cash thus had the opportunity to get out by selling their shares in the market if they so wished.

Responses to rights issues

Companies making rights issues will in due course indicate how well their shareholders have responded. Immediately after the closing date, possibly on the same day, you will see something like this, from bookmaker William Hill:

> William Hill received valid acceptances in respect of 338,922,844 New Ordinary Shares, representing approximately 97.41 per cent of the total number of New Ordinary Shares offered to Shareholders, pursuant to the 1 for 1 Rights Issue.
>
> It is expected that the New Ordinary Shares in uncertificated form will be credited to CREST accounts on 8 April 2009 and that definitive share certificates in respect of New Ordinary Shares in certificated form will be dispatched to Shareholders by no later than 16 April 2009. It is expected that the New Ordinary Shares will commence trading on London Stock Exchange on 8 April 2009.
>
> Citigroup Global Markets will use reasonable endeavours to procure subscribers for the balance of 9,004,597 New Ordinary Shares not validly taken up under the Rights Issue.

Considering that shareholders were asked to buy one new share for every one already held, a pretty hefty imposition, the take-up is staggeringly high, indicating that shareholders have great confidence in the company's future.

Just before the closing date outsider Mon Mome won the Grand National and reports that the bookies had made a killing were splashed in the newspapers, which perhaps encouraged last minute applications.

Hill then tells shareholders when they can expect their shares. CREST is the stock exchange's electronic share register that does away with paper certificates. Those who forgo the comforting pieces of paper get their shares within a day while those who insist on a certificate must wait up to a week for these to be issued.

A date is given when the new shares can be sold on the exchange. This is normally the day after the rights issue closed.

Figure 9.2: William Hill

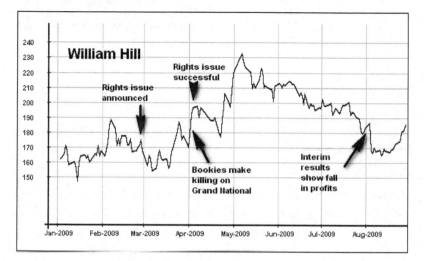

Financial institution Citigroup will now attempt to find buyers for the shares that were rejected in the rights issue. These buyers could be existing shareholders or new ones. Such a placing can depress the share price, as buyers may have to be tempted with a price below the stock market price. The smaller the number of shares that have to be sold, the less effect there will be on the share price.

William Hill's share price had picked up from 110p to 190p in the three months before the rights issue was announced but had fallen back to 155p on concerns over the size of the issue. A fresh surge took them to 197p and they eased back to 190p on the day that the take-up was revealed – on the whole a very satisfactory outcome.

Placings

In a share placing, new shares are offered to large institutional investors rather than to all existing shareholders in proportion to their holdings.

The advantages from the company's point of view is that a placing can be carried out at less cost in a much shorter period of time with a greater certainty of success. It is rare for a placing to fail, so when one is announced it is fair to assume that it will go through (the company and its stock brokers have probably already sounded out major investors to gauge their reaction to a fund raising).

A placing may be accompanied by an open offer, under which existing shareholders are given the opportunity of buying some shares. In this case any requests from existing shareholders are met first. Alternatively the issue may be on a non pre-emptive basis, which means that existing shareholders are frozen out.

Case study: SSL

SSL announced its intention to raise cash through a share issue at a time when other companies were cutting back in the recession. The group has two seemingly unrelated businesses, Durex condoms and Scholl footwear – both of which proved resilient to the economic downturn.

It made this announcement:

> SSL announces its intention to conduct a bookbuilt, non pre-emptive placing of up to 19.19 million new ordinary shares.
>
> The net proceeds, together with existing debt facilities and cash generated from operations, will be used to provide the Company with the financial flexibility to fund its planned medium term organic growth, to pursue selected bolt-on acquisitions, and (if the Board decides that it would be in the Company's best interests to do so) to fund the exercise of an option to increase the Company's shareholding in Beleggingsmaatschappij Lemore to 50% plus one share.

> The Shares are being placed at a price to be determined at the close of the bookbuilding process. The Placing Shares will represent a maximum of 9.99% of the Company's current issued ordinary share capital.

Bookbuilding is where large institutions are asked if they wish to buy shares. If so, they are asked to state how many shares they want and the price they are prepared to pay. In this way the advisers handling the issue can accurately judge the number of shares that can be easily sold and the best price that they can be issued at.

SSL does not give a precise number of shares to be issued, only a maximum. This is because it cannot be certain how well the bookbuilding exercise will go, even if informal soundings have already been taken.

The bookbuilding will be in the hands of City stockbrokers who will act as book runners, which means they will run round the City (by phone rather than on foot!) to drum up interest. It is usual to have two book runners to increase the chances of success.

Reasons for the placing

As a shareholder, you will naturally hope that cash is being raised to expand a successful business rather than to bail out a failure.

SSL makes clear that it is not strapped for cash. It has facilities to borrow from the bank and its existing operations are generating cash. This is reassuring. It wants to build what is often referred to in the press as a *war chest* – a cash pile that can be used to fund growth.

SSL is also clear how the money will be used to fund expansion within the existing operations (organic growth) to pay for comparatively small acquisitions that fit in with the exiting operations and can be 'bolted on' to take majority control of an east European distributor of condoms where it has a 15.5% stake.

Investors may wonder why, if the company is generating cash, it needs to raise money through a share issue. This is explained:

Placing Rationale

The Company has completed a number of acquisitions funded through cash flow and its bank facilities including:

- Crest, the number two condom brand in Switzerland, for £4.6 million;

- a 15.5% shareholding in BLBV, which distributes condoms in the Commonwealth of Independent States markets excluding Ukraine, for £24.6 million;

- the Orthaheel brands, a business based around a range of orthotic insoles, for an initial payment of £14.6 million; and

- the 50% shareholding not already owned in Qingdao London Durex, which manufactures and distributes Durex condoms for the Chinese market, for £19.1 million.

These completed transactions, with an aggregate consideration equivalent to approximately £63 million, are in addition to expansionary capex of £8 million and the expenditure of £26 million in connection with the restructuring of the Group's supply chain.

The Company believes that there may be other opportunities to acquire complementary brands and businesses and to expand into new geographies at attractive prices.

SSL has already been involved in considerable expansion, buying other companies at home and abroad. It has also invested heavily in its existing businesses.

Current trading

An interim management statement accompanying the announcement indicates that 'trading remains in line with expectations' and that 'the performance of Durex and Scholl remains encouraging'. It says that the business continues to grow strongly and while the trading environment is 'unquestionably difficult' the group 'remains confident of achieving its previously stated targets'.

Sales are growing, costs are under control and profits are boosted by the fall in sterling against the euro and Asian currencies. The balance sheet is strong and operating profits are up more than 30%, the trading update claims.

We now have a clear indication of the state of play at SSL so we can assess the impact of the share placing. It seems that the group is on top of its game and we can feel confident that the money raised will bring future benefits. SSL is looking for growth within the markets it understands.

One word of caution: however successful a company has been in expanding, there often comes a point where it overreaches itself. Keep an eye open for the first sign of indigestion.

Result of the placing

Also, watch for a further announcement that will tell you how well the placing has gone. This should happen later the same day or certainly within 48 hours – bookbuilding exercises are usually over quickly and the City's enthusiasm for the shares is reflected in the time it takes to get the issue away.

Before the stock exchange closed that evening, SSL was able to say:

> **Result of Equity Placing**
>
> A total of 19,190,000 new ordinary shares have been placed with institutions at a price of 455p, a discount to the previous closing share price of 2.4 per cent.

The whole issue has been snapped up within hours, which is good news. The placing price is just below the prevailing stock market price but that is no cause for concern. You would expect a discount given that the issue increases the size of the company by 10%. After all, that is a fair wedge of shares to get away and if institutions had been actively looking to increase their holdings in SSL they could have bought shares in the market previously.

Figure 9.3: SSL

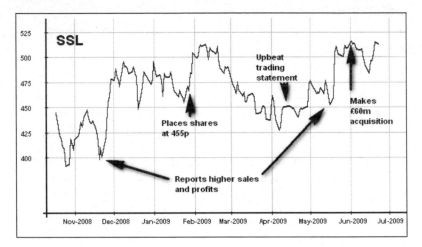

Case study: Tullow Oil

Tullow Oil, an exploration company, issued two statements simultaneously before the stock market opened on January 21, 2009. One was a bullish trading update, the other a fund raising.

It is always worth checking whether there is a second announcement along with any routine one such as results or trading statements. While it is a little messy to have two separate announcements it does mean that an important development is flagged up rather than hidden away at the bottom of a lengthy document.

Usually the trading statement or results will carry a note pointing out that there is another statement, as indeed Tullow's trading statement did. The placing statement said:

> Tullow Oil announces its intention to place up to 66,938,141 new ordinary shares in the Company, representing up to approximately 9.1 per cent of Tullow Oil's existing issued ordinary share capital, with new and existing institutional investors.
>
> The Placing is being conducted through an accelerated book-building process to be carried out by Merrill Lynch and RBS Hoare Govett,

who are acting as joint bookrunners. The number of Placing Shares and the price at which the Placing Shares are to be placed are subject to agreement between Tullow Oil, Merrill Lynch and RBS Hoare Govett at the close of the book-building process. Details of the number of Placing Shares and the Placing Price will be announced as soon as practicable after the close of the book-building process.

The Placing Shares will, when issued, be credited as fully paid and will rank pari passu in all respects with the existing ordinary shares of 10 pence each in the capital of the Company, including the right to receive all dividends and other distributions declared, made or paid on or in respect of such shares after the date of issue of the Placing Shares. The Placing will be made on a non-pre-emptive basis.

We can immediately see some similarities with the placing by SSL. The maximum size, equal to 9-10% of the company is similar. This is roughly the maximum size that can normally be placed comfortably without swamping the market and driving down the placing price.

Again two brokers are acting as bookbuilders. Accelerated means the exercise will be over quickly, usually within a day. The shares will rank pari passu with existing shares which means they will have equal status as soon as they are issued. Existing shareholders will not have the right to buy shares.

Reasons for the placing

We need to know why Tullow is making the placing, though. We want to see positive reasons that will indicate the future prosperity of the company.

Background to the Placing

Tullow's business has continued to perform very strongly in 2008. A 100% exploration success rate was achieved in Ghana and Uganda and overall the Group's exploration drilling programme has resulted in 17 discoveries from 22 wells. Booked Commercial Reserves and Contingent Resources are expected to be upgraded to approximately 800 mmboe at the end of 2008 compared with 551 mmboe a year ago.

It seems that Tullow is not asking for the extra cash out of desperation. Drilling for oil can have a high failure rate, since even promising prospects may prove disappointing, so Tullow's success rate is exceptionally good. Also, in an age of dwindling oil supplies, it is good to see the group's reserves increasing.

Reserves are measured in million of barrels of oil equivalent (mmboe) with any gas being assessed in terms of the equivalent amount of oil. This is normal industry practice.

Tullow goes on to detail progress in its wells, including the Jubilee field in Ghana, adding:

> Phase 1 of the Jubilee development project is now substantially under way. Tullow's existing lending facility, which matures in 2012, is underpinned by a strong syndicate of 18 banks. Tullow has been working very closely with this syndicate and certain new banks to incorporate the first phase of the Ghana Jubilee project, together with the existing production assets, into a new combined facility of up to $2bn. Approval from banks of facilities of $1.15bn is already in place with the remainder of banks well advanced in their internal process.
>
> Tullow will fund Jubilee Phase 1 and existing mature production activities from these debt facilities. However, Tullow is now in the middle of a very exciting period for its Ghanaian and Ugandan operations with further transformational exploration wells to be drilled in the first half of 2009.

So Tullow wants money to fund expansion and further exploration and its bankers are willing to chip in with most of the cash. We can see from the statement that the company is making excellent progress and the outlook is positive. This reading of the situation was confirmed by the 2008 full year results issued at the same time.

Figure 9.4: Tullow

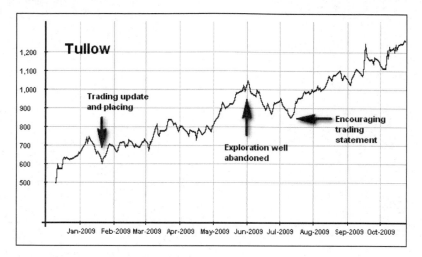

Right at the end of the results statement were details of a conference call to be held on the morning of the announcements with the chief executive, chief operating officer, the exploration director and the chief financial officer all in attendance.

Such a heavyweight line-up is unusual – most conference calls offer only a couple of top directors. It means one of two extremes:

1. the news is particularly good and they all want to bask in the sunlight, or

2. the news is particularly bad and everyone is being wheeled out to repel the critics.

Fortunately it is always pretty obvious which it is. In this case an added clue was that ordinary investors were given the opportunity to phone in. Generally, only analysts and financial journalists are granted this privilege and a company will not widen the scope of an embarrassing exchange.

Details were also given of how to access a recording of the conference call, affording an opportunity for more bashful investors to listen to whether the company executives answered questions frankly or wriggled on a hook.

10.
Changes In Important Shareholdings

An important guide to how well a company is faring can be found in spotting whether directors are buying or selling the shares.

Such purchases and sales must be declared through an official news channel, although they are not seen as being as price sensitive as company results. Also there may be a slight delay while the director informs the company and the company passes the information on to the market. You may not know about the transaction until a day or two after it happens.

Thus director buys and sells are not typically issued at 7am before the market opens. They tend to filter through in the afternoon and many are recorded between the market close at 4.30pm and the closing of the Regulatory News Service at 6.30pm.

Watch out for directors buying on the day that results are announced. There are restrictions on when they can buy and sell; they are not allowed to trade while they are in possession of price sensitive information. The release of results gives them the opportunity to buy or sell if they wish.

We naturally expect newly appointed directors to buy shares as a sign of commitment to the business they are helping to run. Similarly we should not be surprised if a director who quits seeks to reduce his or her holding.

Otherwise the buying and selling of shares by board members is an indication, but not a surefire signal, of how well the company is doing. There is no set formula for how many shares directors should hold between them. Factors such as the size of the company and whether it is still controlled by the founders will influence the percentage of shares in the hands of the board.

Simple statement

If we are lucky we get an admirably straightforward record of a director's deal, as in this case from mining group Lonmin:

> Roger Phillimore, chairman, today bought 15,000 ordinary shares of $1 each in the capital of the Company at an average price of 1438.5281p per share. Upon settlement of this transaction, Mr Phillimore's total holding will be 18,614 shares.

We know instantly who (in this case the chairman) has bought shares, how many shares he has bought, the average price paid and his total shareholding after the purchases. In this case Phillimore presumably bought the shares in several batches, hence the average price running to four decimal places.

Lonmin shares usually trade in batches of 3,000 so the chairman has probably bought in five separate transactions a few seconds apart. With the normal fluctuations in the share price during the trading day he has possibly paid five different prices, each somewhere between 1435p and 1440p.

Incentive plans

It is always better for shareholders if directors buy shares in the company but often they get them free or on the cheap. Most companies have an incentive plan under which a number of shares are awarded to executives each year depending on the performance of the company.

These shares will be issued free or at a fixed price, either now or at some point in the future. The idea is that the directors will be encouraged to see that the share price goes up, so that their awards are more valuable.

Here is a typical announcement from public relations firm Huntsworth:

Directors/PDMR Shareholding

On 23 March 2009 the following awards were made to the executive directors of the Company for nil consideration under the Huntsworth Deferred Share Bonus Plan (the 'Plan').

No. of ordinary shares awarded

Lord Chadlington	1,727,885
Sally Withey	865,385
Tymon Broadhead	346,154

These awards will vest, generally subject to continuing employment, on 23 March 2011 in respect of 50% of the shares and on 23 March 2012 in respect of the remaining 50%.

At the time of these awards the total number of Huntsworth ordinary shares held by each of the directors is:

No. of ordinary shares

Lord Chadlington	3,958,974
Sally Withey	24,356
Tymon Broadhead	18,696

PDMR stands for *persons discharging managerial responsibility*, in other words it includes executives just below board level.

Nil consideration means that the shares were awarded free. Consideration is commonly used by companies to mean the price paid. This is a deferred share bonus plan: the shares awarded are not handed out immediately but at some date in the future.

This means that the directors are encouraged to work hard in the meantime to ensure the success of the company and hence a rise in the share price. It also means that the directors are encouraged to stay until the date that the shares are 'vested', that is actually handed over. Leaving the company in the meantime means that any shares not yet vested will be lost.

In this particular case half the shares are to be vested in two years time and the rest 12 months later.

We can see from the second table that Lord Chadlington already has a substantial shareholding while the other two executives will see their holdings boosted many times over by the bonus shares.

Selling incentive shares

Alas, most directors would rather have cash than shares so they will often sell shares granted under an incentive scheme as soon as they lay their hands on them.

Where a director sells shares we should therefore check whether he or she is reducing their holding or simply cashing in their incentive awards.

Understanding the form

We have looked at simple, easy to understand announcements of directors' deals but unfortunately companies often tend to reproduce the complex form that they fill in to register the transaction with the LSE.

Do not be put off by all the daunting questions. Most will be left blank or marked N/A for not applicable. It looks like this:

Directors' Dealing Form

1. Name of the issuer
    A.G.BARR

2. State whether the notification relates to (i) a transaction
    notified in accordance with DR 3.1.4R(1)(a); or
    (ii) DR 3.1.4(R)(1)(b) a disclosure made in accordance with
    section 324 (as extended by section 328) of the Companies
    Act 1985; or (iii) both (i) and (ii)
    both (i) and (ii)

3. Name of person discharging managerial responsibilities/
    director
    A B C Short

4. State whether notification relates to a person connected with
    a person discharging managerial responsibilities/director
    named in 3 and identify the connected person

5. Indicate whether the notification is in respect of a holding of
    the person referred to in 3 or 4 above or in respect of a non-
    beneficial interest
    Non-beneficial as Trustee

6. Description of shares (including class), debentures or
    derivatives or financial instruments relating to shares
    Ordinary 25p

7. Name of registered shareholders(s) and, if more than one, the
    number of shares held by each of them
    Trustee – The A.G.BARR Profit Linked Share Plan

8   State the nature of the transaction
    Share Purchase

9. Number of shares, debentures or financial instruments relating to shares acquired
   134

10. Percentage of issued class acquired (treasury shares of that class should not be taken into account when calculating percentage)
    0.001%

11. Number of shares, debentures or financial instruments relating to shares disposed

12. Percentage of issued class

13. Price per share or value of transaction
    £12.56

14. Date and place of transaction
    7 May 2009

15. Total holding following notification and total percentage holding following notification (any treasury shares should not be taken into account when calculating percentage)
    58,284 – 0.30%

16. Date issuer informed of transaction
    08 May 2009

What this means

We are not bothered about the various regulations specified in question 2. Leave the company secretary to worry about that. What we see here is that a director of soft drinks company A.G.Barr named ABC Short has acquired 134 ordinary shares at £12.56 each and that they represent a tiny fraction of one per cent of the total number of Barr's shares. He now has 58,284 shares, still only one third of one per cent.

If we want to know who Short is we have to check the company website to discover that Alex Short is the finance director. And he hasn't bought the shares himself. They have been bought for him by the company scheme to issue shares to directors as an incentive. Hence the reference to the shares being held by a trustee rather than the beneficial (real) owner.

Changes in large shareholdings

It is worth noting that a similarly daunting but reasonably understandable form is used for purchases or sales by large shareholders. These notifications keep you abreast of possible takeovers or warn you that an important investor is getting out. You will see something like this, from software group Invensys:

TR-1: Notifications of Major Interests in Shares	
1. Identity of the issuer or the underlying issuer of existing shares to which voting rights are attached:	Invensys plc
2. Reason for notification (yes/no)	
An acquisition or disposal of voting rights	yes
An acquisition or disposal of financial instruments which may result in the acquisition of shares already issued to which voting rights are attached	no
An event changing the breakdown of voting rights	no
Other (please specify):	no
3. Full name of person(s) subject to notification obligation:	Standard LIfe Investments Ltd
4. Full name of shareholder(s) (if different from 3):	Vidacos Nominees
5. Date of transaction (and date on which the threshold is crossed or reached if different):	6 May 2009
6. Date on which issuer notified:	7 May 2009
7. Threshold(s) that is/are crossed or reached:	13%
8. Notified Details	
A. Voting rights attached to shares	
Class/type of share. If possible use ISIN code	GB00B19DVX61

Situation previous to the triggering transaction				
Number of shares	Number of voting rights			
104,259,376	104,259,376			
Resulting situation after the triggering transaction				
Number of shares	Number of voting rights		Percentage of voting rights	
	Direct	Indirect	Direct	Indirect
104,173,202	58,483,782	45,689,420	7.297%	5.701%
B. Financial Instruments				
Resulting situation after the triggering transaction				
Type of financial instrument	Expiration date	Exercise/ conversion period/date	No. of voting rights that may be acquired (if the instrument exercised/ converted)	Percentage of voting rights
Total (A+B)				
Number of voting rights	Percentage of voting rights			
104,173,202	12.998%			

This refers to a transaction by fund manager Standard Life through a nominee company. Look carefully and you will see that Standard has sold a small number of shares. It had 104,259,376 shares previously and now has 104,173,202, which is 86,174 fewer. This has taken its holding below 13%.

11.

Board Changes

The resignation of a director is always a matter of potential concern, though the reasons may be entirely innocent and no cause for alarm. Consider these issues:

1. How important is the director?

2. How long has he or she been on the board?

3. Why are they going?

4. Is there a replacement ready to step into the vacant position?

Order of importance

The two directors most likely to be missed are the chairman and chief executive. These are the top two posts on any board and the departure leaves a hole that needs filling pronto.

It is possible, for a short time, for either the chairman or chief executive to take on a dual role or for a senior executive to act as makeshift chief executive but this puts a considerable strain on the individuals carrying the burden and risks leaving the ship effectively rudderless.

Then comes the finance director, a key post in any organisation.

Next in line are other executives such as the marketing director or sales director. These are important posts, which is why the occupant is on the board in the first place, but it is easier to replace someone on the second or third rung of management rather than the top.

Last in the order of worry are the non-executives. These do not take an active part in the day-to-day running of the business and will probably do no more than attend monthly board meetings to offer advice based on their experience in business. They have the least influence on the success of the company and are most easily replaced.

Length of service

The length of time that a director has been on board is a double edged weapon: a long serving director will have vast experience of the business but may have gone stale and run out of ideas; short-term directors will have less knowledge of the business but it sends out a warning if they cannot settle in.

As a general rule, the departure of a long serving chief executive or chairman is a negative sign. Either the business is losing a successful key person who will be a hard act to follow or it is getting rid of a deadbeat, leaving someone else to pick up the pieces.

The departure of a long-serving non-executive is a positive sign. Non-executives are supposed to point out flaws in the company's strategy or suggest new directions. The longer they serve, the more pally they get with the executives and cease to be an effective alternative voice.

If a director quits or is ousted soon after joining the board, this is always a negative sign. Whether the director jumps or is pushed, it looks as if the wrong person was appointed, which reflects badly on all parties concerned.

It is possible that another post has been offered to the director that would create a clash of interests but what does that say about the company he or she is quitting after a short tenure? The implication is that the other company is more attractive to work for.

Why are they going?

The company statement will usually offer some explanation of why the director is leaving, although the reasons given may be unconvincing or downright woolly. Be particularly suspicious if you do not feel satisfied with the explanation.

Phrases such as 'leaving to pursue other interests' or 'looking for a new challenge' simply mean that the director has left without another job to go to. One should wonder not only why they are going, especially in the case of an executive who is losing a full-time salary, but also why the company feels unable to offer a cogent reason.

It could mean internal strife within the board, a power struggle between two strong characters or a clash over the direction the company should be going in. Internal divisions in any structure are weakening. If issues cannot be resolved civilly then trouble is being stored up for the future.

Another possibility is that one strong wilful character is clearing out voices of reason.

The most acceptable reason is that the director is retiring. This will have been known about for some time so it should be possible to announce a successor in the same breath and ensure continuity. Ideally a replacement will overlap the outgoing director to learn the ropes. A proposed new chairman will often serve as vice-chairman for a few months.

An internal replacement is generally advantageous in the case of an executive director, particularly if the company is a successful one. For example, a finance director who has run a tight ship and knows the company well is likely to make a decent chief executive, although there are no guarantees in this life.

Forward planning takes all the anguish out of changes in key directorships, giving an impression of stability and continuity.

Case study: Associated British Foods

As a simple example of how to do it properly, we can use Associated British Foods as a template. As its name implies, ABF is mainly a food producer with products including cereals, hot beverages, sugars, vegetable oils, bread and bakery ingredients. More recently it diversified into retailing, mainly through the Primark budget chain.

The two strands of the business are not obviously compatible. One is in retail, the other in supplying retailers; one is in food and the other in clothing and household goods; the food part operates world wide while the retail side is in just four European countries. Anyone at the helm needs a good grasp of both parts.

On 3 September 2008, ABF issued a simple statement:

Directorate change

Associated British Foods is pleased to announce the appointment of Charles Sinclair as an independent non-executive director, from 1 October 2008. Charles Sinclair is currently chief executive of Daily Mail and General Trust plc but will be retiring from this role on the 30 September 2008.

Charles Sinclair is a non-executive director of SVG Capital.

This was a low-key announcement causing little excitement. The appointment of a non-executive is pretty routine. As per stock exchange requirements, details of his other directorships were given so that shareholders would know something of his background.

Sinclair duly settled in on October 1 and got to know the business and the rest of the board. Once it was clear that he was up to scratch, ABF made a follow-up announcement:

Directorate change

Associated British Foods plc announces that Martin Adamson has today notified his intention to retire from the Board on 21 April 2009. Charles Sinclair, a non-executive Director of the Company since 1 October 2008, will succeed Martin Adamson as non-executive Chairman.

Adamson had joined the board in 1999, becoming chairman three years later. He knew he was approaching 60 years of age, and was no doubt conscious of the possibility of retiring and making way for new blood. This was all done in an orderly fashion that guaranteed a minimum of upheaval in what is, after all, one of the top two posts in any company.

Case study: Johnston Press

It looked as if newspaper publishing group Johnston Press was also managing a smooth handover when it made this announcement on 5 January 2009:

Board Change

Johnston Press, one of the leading regional media groups in the UK and Ireland, announces that John Fry has today joined the Company as its new Chief Executive and has also been appointed as a Director. He replaces Tim Bowdler, who stands down as Chief Executive and a Director of Johnston Press in anticipation of his planned retirement in May 2009 after 15 years with the Company. Mr Bowdler will be retained by Johnston Press for a period to assist in a smooth transfer of responsibilities.

However, Fry's arrival did not run smoothly. The trouble with making outside appointments of chief executives is that they tend to waltz in and make sweeping changes to stamp their mark on the business.

Within a month, Johnston Press was subject to further upheaval, as this follow-up announcement shows:

Board changes

Roger Parry, Simon Waugh and Gavin Patterson to leave the Board

Ian Russell appointed Chairman

Johnston Press announces that Ian Russell will succeed Roger Parry as Chairman with effect from 12 March 2009. Simon Waugh will be leaving the Board with effect from 30 January 2009. Roger Parry and Gavin Patterson will not be seeking re-election/election at the AGM.

Changing both top directors in such a short space of time can cause considerable disruption. As the announcement went on to say, Russell had been on the board for less than two years. To lose two other directors in rapid succession only adds to the uncertainty.

Background

This was in sharp contrast to the background to Fry's appointment: the search for a new chief executive had taken 18 months. Shareholders were entitled to wonder about the apparent reticence of suitable candidates to sit on the board of a company that had expanded to become the second largest regional newspaper publisher in the UK and the largest publisher of weekly newspapers in the Republic of Ireland.

Admittedly, there was an element of misfortune in the departure of three directors at virtually the same time. Parry had been on the board for 12 years, eight of them as chairman, so he had put in a fair stint. He had led the search for a new chief executive, a task that was now complete.

Waugh had just been appointed the first chief executive of the new National Apprenticeship Service and Patterson, like Waugh a non-executive, had been promoted at his day job at telecoms group BT.

Figure 11.1: Johnston Press

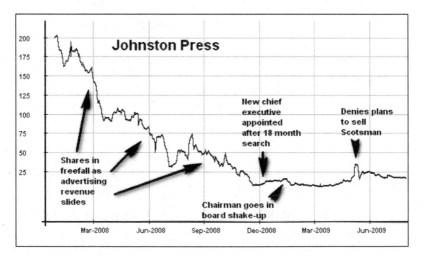

The departures left Johnston Press with three vacancies for non-executive directors out of seven, potentially leaving the four executives forming a majority on the board.

The newspaper industry was in turmoil with readership generally falling as young readers switched to the internet and advertising slumping not only because of the economic downturn but also because advertisers were switching to other media.

It was reasonable to consider whether the departing non-executives had been influenced in their decision by a looming strategy review that could lead to sweeping changes. Shareholders needed to decide if it was advantageous for Fry to be effectively given free rein to make painful but necessary changes or whether an experienced, steadying hand was needed to offer alternative ideas.

Gushing tributes

Top level arrivals and departures are usually accompanied with praise for the individuals concerned, ranging from polite to obsequious. A liberal sprinkling of forenames gives an impression of warm cuddliness among those who run the company.

The departing worthies express what an honour it has been to work for such a wonderful company run by such jolly good chaps while the incoming executive is equally enthused about taking the company on its next great leap forward.

The only exception is when someone has been ousted, and even then there is often some face-saving form of words.

Do not assume because some acclaimed global giant has deigned to take the reins at a company you are interested in that the fortunes will be transformed overnight. Nor does the departure of an apparent genius who has allegedly transformed the business mean the end of the world.

As always, view fulsome praise with a critical eye.

As an example of gushing prose, these words accompanied the announcement of the impending departure of Mark Tucker as chief executive of insurance group Prudential and the appointment of his replacement Tidjane Thiam. (Have the sick bag ready.)

Harvey McGrath, Prudential Chairman, said:

'Mark has made an outstanding contribution and has led the transformation of Prudential into the strongest, and best focused, company in the sector with a diversified international presence in advantaged regions and markets. He is a world-class leader and we are very grateful to have had his leadership, vision, drive and commitment. We are truly sorry to see him go, but fully respect his decision.

Tidjane is ideally equipped to succeed Mark, given his global experience, knowledge of the sector and his outstanding leadership qualities. We are delighted to have such an outstanding and proven successor in Tidjane.'

Commenting, Mark Tucker said:

'Choosing to leave Prudential has been one of the hardest decisions of my life. When I was appointed Group Chief Executive here, I set myself a number of key deliverables – namely establishing a clear and readily understood strategy that would deliver sustainable growth, improving the overall quality of our business through selective disposals, building the best executive team in the industry, driving continually improving performance and ensuring that world class leadership succession was in place. I believe that I have delivered on what I set out to do and that the time is now right to hand over to a successor to continue the work.

I am deeply proud of what the team here at Prudential has delivered and believe that we have in place very firm foundations for the next phase of Prudential's growth. I am excited by the quality of my successor, Tidjane, who I know will do an outstanding job.'

Commenting, Tidjane Thiam, Chief Financial Officer, said:

'I am delighted at this opportunity. Prudential is an outstanding organisation, with a proud history and an exciting future. Mark is an outstanding Chief Executive, who has transformed Prudential into a strategically focused, efficient and very strongly capitalised business. It will be a privilege to work with the Executive team to lead Prudential into its next stage of development.'

Take all instances of this sort of stuff with a pinch of salt. It is all too common and all too meaningless. As a general rule, the more gushing the tributes the more sceptical you should be. A short thank you and welcome to the individuals concerned is quite sufficient.

Abrupt departures

However, one has to admit that an amicable parting is far better than a curt goodbye.

This statement issued by Rio Tinto is a masterpiece of unhelpfulness, offering no explanation for an extraordinary turn of events. Indeed the tone of the announcement is matter of fact, as if some minor issue of no consequence had occurred.

Mr Jim Leng

Rio Tinto announces that Jim Leng, a non-executive Director, has resigned from the Boards with immediate effect and will therefore not take up the post of Chairman of the Boards in April as previously planned.

At the request of the Boards, Rio Tinto's current Chairman, Paul Skinner, has agreed to remain as Chairman until mid 2009, by which time it is anticipated that a successor will be appointed. The process to appoint a new Chairman is underway.

And that was it, apart from a couple of paragraphs saying that Rio Tinto was an international mining company and summarising its business activities.

Bad as it is for a chairman to quit soon after his appointment, it is doubly embarrassing that he should go without even taking up the post. This was not just a run-of-the-mill non-executive who could easily be replaced but the man brought in specifically to head the group.

His appointment a month earlier had been embellished with a rather more effusive announcement proclaiming that he:

---

brings to Rio Tinto extensive industrial company experience and is a seasoned Board room operator. He is ably qualified to lead Rio Tinto into the next phase of its development.

Yet on his resignation Rio Tinto felt no need to enlighten shareholders, who were forced to consult websites or the following day's newspapers to find out what was going on. No hint of whether there was a disagreement over strategy, a clash of personalities or whatever, nor any indication of whether Leng was entitled to a payoff for any inconvenience suffered.

Even Leng, who had been appointed to the board only a month earlier, felt unable to assist the people who, after all, owned the business. He subsequently issued a personal statement claiming that the board's strategy 'has never been questioned' as it had 'served its shareholders exceedingly well in the past'.

Surely the incoming chairman should question the existing strategy. That is one of the things he is appointed to do. What has served well in the past may not do so in the future.

Then Leng referred enigmatically to Rio's 'attempts to resolve its issues' and his hope that the board would reach 'a consensual decision'. Hold on a minute. What issues? There weren't supposed to be any. A consensus on what? There is no hint of a disagreement on anything in the bland company statement.

Background to the turmoil

In fact, as financial journalists and City speculation revealed, there was a serious boardroom split over how to service the group's £25 billion debt: whether to make a rights issue, sell assets or accept an investment from the Aluminium Corporation of China. These remedies had implications for investors.

Rio Tinto had run up most of its debt buying Canadian aluminium group Alcan at the height of the commodities boom. The burden was a key reason for rival BHP Billiton to drop a proposed takeover of Rio.

Investors confused over what was going on may well have looked at the recent performance of Rio's share price, which had soared during the commodity boom but tumbled more rapidly when the bubble burst.

Figure 11.2: Rio Tinto

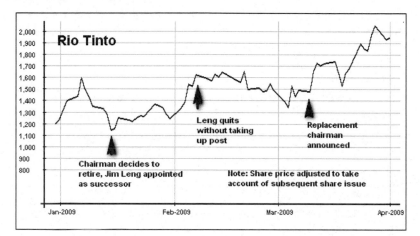

It took four years for the shares to get from £13 to £70 in May 2008 but only seven months to dip below £10. There had been some recovery to around £20 at the time Leng was ousted, with some investors feeling that the sell-off had been overdone, but they fell 2% to £19.20 that day.

Despite its status as a member of the FTSE 100 elite, Rio looked a decidedly speculative investment until funding issues could be settled, not to mention the appointment of a new chairman.

Return of former directors

Sometimes ghosts in the form of previous directors come back to haunt companies. While that can certainly be scary for the incumbent board, it may be spiritually uplifting for shareholders.

It is not unusual for the founder of a company to build up his pet project into a major concern, listing his company on the stock market somewhere along the way to raise cash for expansion.

However, at some point the founder bows out voluntarily or is ousted. Perhaps the company has outgrown him and he is no longer the man to be at the helm (we refer to 'he' in this context because it is invariably a male); his company may have been taken over by a larger rival; he may have diluted his shareholding by issuing new shares for acquisitions, which means he can be outvoted by other shareholders.

Such people do have a tendency to hold onto a substantial holding in order to share the benefits of the company that they set up and built. They often look for a way back, so any decision by a former director to buy or sell shares in a company can be an important signal of intent.

Case study: Redrow

An excellent example is the case of house builder Redrow, which issued this statement:

Bridgemere Board Proposal

Redrow has been notified by Mr Steve Morgan that, through his investment vehicle Bridgemere Securities, he has increased his direct holding from 16.96 per cent to 23.46 per cent of the issued share capital of Redrow. The board has been advised by Mr Morgan that he purchased these additional shares from Toscafund Asset Management. The board has also been advised by Mr Morgan that Bridgemere holds contracts for difference over an additional 6.46 per cent and Bridgemere would therefore have an interest in approximately 29.9 per cent of the issued share capital of Redrow if these contracts were closed out through physical settlement.

Mr Morgan has proposed that he should join the board of Redrow in an executive role which, together with other proposals, would result in a fundamental change in the composition of the board. The board remains committed to its high standards of corporate governance and is seeking clarity on these board changes and other critical aspects of Mr Morgan's proposal.

In separate announcements, both Bridgemere and Toscafund confirmed the change in their shareholdings.

Morgan founded Redrow in 1974 at the age of 21. He floated the company on the stock exchange in 1994 and stepped down as chairman in 2000. No doubt he still thought of it as his baby and no doubt it would have troubled him to see his baby suffering in someone else's care in the sharp downturn in the housing market during the credit crunch.

The existence of substantial shareholdings between 10% and 30% in a company are always of particular interest to other investors. Such holdings are large enough to provide a springboard for a bid but not large enough to give control of the company.

Morgan, with just under 17%, and investment fund Toscafund with 27%, both had substantial holdings in Redrow without having control. Here we had an announcement that involved one selling shares to the other.

The reference to Morgan's 'direct' holding means that these are shares that he actually owned, albeit through his own investment vehicle. He also potentially owned shares indirectly through contracts for difference (CFDs).

Up to 2003 it was not necessary for substantial shareholders to declare that they held contracts for difference. The rules were changed after an outcry because potential bidders were effectively increasing their holdings in target companies without declaring the fact. Holders of more than 3% of a company's shares must now declare the purchase or sale of CFDs just as they must declare changes in direct shareholdings as part of the rules regulating takeovers.

This greater transparency means we can see that Morgan has taken his direct stake plus CFDs he has bought to 29.9% of the company, the maximum level he is allowed without having to make a full bid for Redrow under the Takeover Code.

He has also asked for an executive role and it is highly unlikely that he would settle for less than chief executive. Why come back from retirement unless he wanted to run the company again? If he merely wished to play elder statesman at the age of 56 he could have asked to be appointed as a non-executive.

Implications

The implication is that Morgan is backing his horses both ways: that he hopes to gain control of Redrow without the expense of making a bid. On the other hand, if the incumbents resist him, he has the option of bidding.

In the event of a bid, it is likely that he would have the support of Toscafund, which has very conveniently sold to him exactly the number of shares that he wanted. The two holdings combined would amount to just over half the shares.

Pressure is now on the Redrow board and they are sensibly asking Morgan what his intensions are and are also asking other major shareholders how they feel about the situation. After all, if Morgan and Toscafund vote together at the AGM they can vote out existing directors and propose replacements.

The potential return of Morgan was well received by investors. Redrow shares had fallen from a peak of 700p at the beginning of 2007 to around 122p after it reported a loss of £46.2 million in the six months to 31st December 2008. News of Morgan's possible return sent them up to 163p and some investors took the opportunity to sell out.

Figure 11.3: Redrow

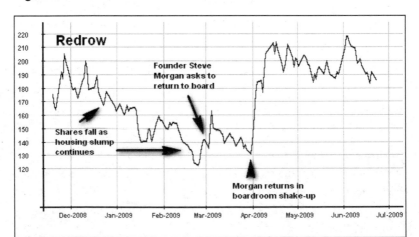

One point to note is that Morgan may well have got his timing right. He knows house building in general and Redrow in particular, so he has an excellent chance of catching the shares at the bottom of the cycle. Probably he thinks that the housing market is turning and that Redrow shares will outperform the stock market, especially if he is in charge. Incidentally, this scenario has implications for other house builders, whose battered shares could also be due for recovery.

Redrow shares perked up 15p to 150p on the day his share purchase was announced. Shareholders did not have long to wait for the outcome. Less than three weeks later the Redrow board capitulated:

Board Changes

Steve Morgan has been appointed to the Board as Deputy Chairman and Chairman designate, acting in an executive capacity.

Following consultation with leading shareholders of the Company, the Board and Mr Morgan have agreed a structure which will allow Mr Morgan to bring his extensive knowledge of the UK housebuilding industry to Redrow and ensure sufficient continuity of the Board and its practices to serve the interests of all shareholders.

Alan Bowkett, Chairman of Redrow, will stand down at the end of Redrow's fiscal year. At this date, Mr Morgan will take on the role of Chairman, acting in an executive capacity.

Neil Fitzsimmons, Chief Executive, and the Board consider it essential that Mr Morgan is afforded the most effective executive structure to take the Company forward. It has therefore been agreed that Mr Fitzsimmons will stand down as Chief Executive. The other executive directors, Group Finance Director David Arnold and regional chairmen Colin Lewis and John Tutte, will remain on the Board and will all report directly to Mr Morgan.

12.

Other Non-routine Issues

Strategic reviews

Often quite out of the blue a company will announce a strategic review under which it will consider all its operations and decide which ones to concentrate on and which, if any, to ditch.

Strategic reviews are often announced when a new chief executive takes over. In such cases one should not put too much store by them. The review probably has more to do with the newcomer's need to get to grips with the business as with any actual need for a review.

They are also common when a company is in difficulties, partly because the mess needs sorting out and partly because the review buys time as shareholders become restless. The announcement of a strategic review in such cases is a signal that problems exist; it may also be a signal that the problems are being addressed, though that is rather less certain.

Just occasionally it really is time for a board to pause and take stock of the situation. Possibly the company has grown over the years and there is some advantage in considering whether all the parts fit together.

The longer a review takes, the more worried investors should be. A review stretching over several months may indicate that the problems are more deep-seated or that there are no obvious solutions.

Case study: Friends Provident

Having seen its share price battered and a potential merger fall through, insurance group Friends Provident embarked on a strategic review to decide what direction the group should take.

The answer, released at the end of January 2008, was to concentrate on its traditional insurance markets. Within the announcement of the outcome of the review was this paragraph:

> The Group owns three businesses which do not fit the revised strategy. They are: F&C Asset Management, Lombard and Pantheon Financial. These businesses are profitable and attractive. The Board intends to explore opportunities for these businesses with a view to maximising value for shareholders. Any capital that is released as a result of these strategies will be returned to shareholders.

The largest and most important of these three unwanted businesses is undoubtedly F&C, which manages assets for wealthy people and runs investment vehicles such as pension funds.

FP owns 52% of F&C, with the minority 48% of shares traded on the London Stock Exchange. F&C has been an albatross, never living up to expectations since FP took a majority stake and dragging down the group. The description of 'attractive' is a blatant sales pitch.

FP does not put a price on any of these three companies, or on what they might make in total, although it is quite common in these circumstances to float an optimistic price tag in the press.

Beware of taking any such valuations seriously. Any company that decides to put part of its business up for sale is immediately in a poorer bargaining position than one that receives an approach from a willing buyer.

If more than one potential buyer emerges quickly, all well and good but monitor potential sales such as this if you own shares in the parent company. The longer that silence reigns, the less likely it is that a sale will be achieved at a decent price.

This is important because the FP announcement makes clear that the proceeds will be handed to shareholders, most likely in the shape of a special one-off dividend. Maximising value for shareholders involves deciding if the proceeds of a sale are more attractive than future profits from continued ownership.

What happened

In the event, the silence was deafening. FP was trying to sell during the credit crunch when potential buyers of companies were circling for fallen victims and attractive sales prices were hard to come by, especially for a company in the finance sector.

Thus, 14 months later, came the admission of failure:

> Both FP and F&C have held discussions with a number of parties concerning a possible transaction involving F&C. Those discussions have now ceased.
>
> FP intends to make a pro-rata distribution of its stake in F&C to its shareholders during 2009. Further information on this distribution will be provided in due course.

This means that instead of receiving cash, Friends Provident shareholders will have the 52% stake in F&C divided up amongst them in proportion to their shareholdings in FP, and F&C will then become a completely independent company.

Debt restructuring

Where a company renegotiates its debt, it is important to consider the reasons and the effects on the company's profits. Debt restructuring can be a boon, a potential disaster or a cloud with a silver lining.

Most companies work with various forms of borrowings intended to fund the day to day workings of the business and to finance capital projects. There will probably be an overdraft facility to fund stock levels and to pay suppliers until goods are sold plus a larger, fixed term arrangement.

This is similar to an ordinary individual having an overdraft to get by with while cash is a bit stretched and a 25-year mortgage to buy a house.

Companies may also be favoured with revolving loans, a cross between an overdraft and a term loan. Revolving loans are for a set period but are normally renewed automatically or have a set notice period for termination by the banks.

Terms for the loans vary. They can be fixed at a set percentage for the term of the loan. Overdraft rates tend to be a number of percentage points above the Bank of England's base rate. Loans may also be linked to LIBOR (the London inter-bank offered rate, which is the rate at which banks lend to each other), EurIbor (the Eurozone equivalent) or Nybor (the US version).

Companies quite commonly borrow from more than one bank at the same time. Having the support of a syndicate of banks providing one pot of cash between them is a safeguard in case one wants to pull out, and the banks themselves feel happier at sharing the risk. Loans from just one bank are known as 'bilateral'.

A company may borrow from a syndicate and also have bilateral loans in place. Again, this is perfectly normal and all the lenders will know the state of play and will have agreed to lend money in the full knowledge of the company's total commitments.

Another common form of debt is corporate bonds. These are IOUs issued mainly to banks, other financial institutions and ordinary shareholders. They pay a fixed rate of interest and are to be redeemed at a set date.

Manageable limits

There is nothing wrong with debt, as long as it is manageable. Some businesses would be severely constrained if they had to struggle on without financial backing from their banks. For example, high levels of debt are the norm in sectors such as property development and plant hire, where considerable expense is required up front.

However, banks do tend to hold all the aces where lending is concerned. An overdraft can be cancelled and term loans, unlike standard mortgages, tend to be for just two or three years, rarely more than five, before they come up for renewal.

Furthermore, banks tend to impose terms, known as covenants, which if breached allow the banks to call in the loan early. Typically covenants may demand that the net worth of the company (assets and cash minus borrowings) should not fall below a certain percentage of net debt (debts minus cash in hand) or that profits should be greater than interest payments.

Thus, companies can be required to pay back loans just when they can least afford to do so.

The renegotiating of a loan may simply be because the allotted time span has expired and a new agreement needs to be put in place. Companies with strong profits and cash flow may take the opportunity to negotiate better terms, especially if they were in a position of weakness last time round and were forced to accept draconian terms to secure the continued support of their banks.

On the other hand, the company may be going cap in hand to the banks because it has broken the covenants. This will be expensive. The company will have to stand its own costs in the renegotiations, including the charges of its financial advisers, and pay for the banks' time for however long the talks last. Then the banks will raise the rate of interest they charge.

Case study: SEGRO

Have a look at this announcement from SEGRO, a property group providing space for businesses in Europe:

> **Amendment To Covenant Levels Successfully Achieved**
>
> SEGRO has signed agreements with syndicate banks and bilateral lenders that provide £1.7 billion of debt (drawn and undrawn) to permanently increase the maximum gearing covenant (net debt to net worth) in these facilities, from 125% to 160%. Interest cover covenants, which require net rental income to cover net interest charges by 1.25 times, remain the same.
>
> The Group continues to operate within all of its debt covenants even without the amendments, but in the current uncertain economic environment and difficult property market conditions, SEGRO believes that the amendments provide valuable additional headroom to the Company.

As part of the agreements, SEGRO will pay a one-off fee of £8.6m and the weighted average margin over LIBOR and EURIBOR on these credit facilities at the date of signing will increase by approximately 110 basis points over the previous margin levels. The immediate impact of such increased margins would be to increase the weighted average cost of the Group's debt from approximately 5.20% to 5.75% per annum. However, SEGRO believes the present low interest rate environment provides an opportunity to mitigate most, if not all, of this increased cost.

Note first of all the positive spin in the headline and first paragraph. This is presented as a success story with SEGRO negotiating less onerous terms for its loans. Curiously, the second paragraph begins by pointing out that SEGRO was actually complying with the existing terms. At this point shareholders are entitled to wonder what the fuss is all about.

Having been softened up, shareholders can now be told that SEGRO has had to act because it is quite likely to breach the covenants some time soon (although it is not spelt out anything like as bluntly as that). Still, it is sensible to act in good time rather than be forced to negotiate after the damage is done.

SEGRO now has 'headroom' which means the gap between its current gearing and the maximum allowed.

Paragraph three springs the nasty news: the cost. SEGRO has had to fork out £8.5 million up front as well as paying a higher rate of interest to compensate the banks for taking on an increased risk.

SEGRO had already warned shareholders that it was 'assessing its financing options' and a week later it announced a massive rights issue in which shareholders were invited to buy 12 new shares for every one already held.

Case study: Shanks

Bank refinancing can be a mixed blessing. While it is always good news that a company has finance in place for some time into the future, we should consider on what terms that financing has been agreed, especially if the company is negotiating from a position of weakness.

Waste disposal company Shanks, which has operations in the UK, Netherlands, Belgium and Canada, made this announcement:

> Shanks has signed an agreement to re-finance its £250 million core bank facility. The new facility is a Euro 360 million facility expiring in April 2012 provided by a club comprising six banks. The Group is particularly pleased to have expanded and strengthened its core relationship-banking group in such a difficult funding market.
>
> The new facility is denominated in Euros, but can also be drawn in Sterling or Canadian Dollars. The cost of the facility, both in terms of the up-front arrangement fees and interest margin over LIBOR, although significantly higher than in the past, is in line with current market norms.

The good news is:

- a refinancing has been achieved

- the amount of money available has increased from £250 million to the equivalent of £324 million at the prevailing exchange rate

- six banks, more than before, have been persuaded to lend

- the loan will run for three years, giving Shanks time to get its finances in better order

The bad news is:

- the banks have charged a hefty upfront fee just to put the arrangements in place

- the rate of interest is higher than on the existing loan

Now consider what this announcement does not tell you:

1. how many banks were involved in the existing loan

2. how long the existing loan ran for

3. why a new loan is needed at this time

4. why a loan priced in sterling has been replaced by one in euros

5. what upfront fee was charged and how that compared with the previous equivalent charge

6. what the new rate of interest is and how much higher that is than interest on the existing loan

The fact that Shanks has renegotiated terms in line with what everyone else is having to pay is little consolation. There are huge gaps in our knowledge and we should be correspondingly cautious.

Figure 12.1: Shanks

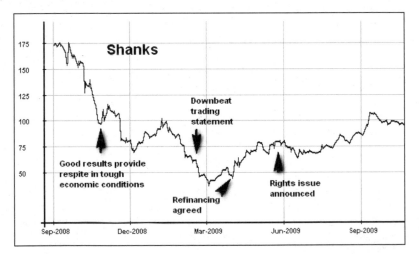

At the last count Shanks had net debts of £388.9 million, mostly on variable interest rates that have risen further above LIBOR, the benchmark rate at which loans to companies are normally linked. It is worrying, then, that the new loans will be even higher.

It is not unreasonable for Shanks to borrow in euros. According to its most recently published results, about three quarters of its revenue comes from the Netherlands and Belgium and these are the fastest growing parts of the group. Companies with international operations should try to match their debts to their income.

However, Shanks's debt, again according to past pronouncements, is already predominantly in euros. That will be fine if the pound recovers and UK income can help to service euro loans but will be a strain if the pound falls, as Shanks recorded in its previous trading statement.

Contract wins and losses

As the move towards greater disclosure has gathered momentum, companies have increasingly seen the advantages in terms of public relations in announcing positive – if not necessarily earth-shattering – developments that are part of their everyday business.

Thus, it is quite common now for contract wins to be paraded in all their glory. Sometimes the contract has not even been won yet. Beware of giveaway phrases such as 'preferred bidder' or 'preferred partner'. The deal is not yet signed and sealed.

The following deal was real enough:

> Costain has been awarded a £397 million contract to design and build municipal waste treatment infrastructure as part of the Greater Manchester Waste Disposal Authority's Waste and Recycling Contract, which is the largest municipal waste contract in Western Europe.
>
> The project, which will cost £3 billion to complete, will treat 1.3 million tonnes of municipal waste annually. The project comprises the design, construction and commissioning of a total of 44 facilities spread across 26 locations.
>
> Serving a resident population of over 2 million people, GMWDA is the largest waste disposal authority in England. It provides waste

> disposal services to approximately 958,000 households across Bolton, Bury, Manchester, Oldham, Rochdale, Salford, Stockport, Tameside and Trafford, and handles around 5% of the UK's national municipal waste.

They do say that where there's muck there's brass and in this case there is nearly £400 million in brass for engineering and construction group Costain.

What does the company get out of it?

Sift what is relevant from the irrelevant. We are not bothered what the whole project will cost as Costain is not putting up the money, nor how many households are included. We are interested in what Costain gets out of it.

Before we get too excited, we check Costain's annual turnover to get some idea of the importance of this contract. Latest figures show turnover at £902 million, so this is a decent deal – although it is a one-off figure, not an annual payment.

The good, the indifferent and the ugly

However, news on contracts is not always positive. One company's gain may be another company's loss. Take this news, issued in March 2009 by newspaper and magazine distributor Dawson Holdings:

> **Contracts renewal process**
>
> Frontline and Seymour Distribution, two clients in the magazine distribution sector, have now advised us that, when their contracts with us expire in April 2010, they will not be renewed. We are clearly very disappointed and will be taking such actions as are necessary to protect our position. The contracts have just over 12 months left to run, thus enabling Dawson to initiate contingency plans in part mitigation of the potential long term financial impact. The impact on the current financial year is not expected to be significant.
>
> In the year ended 27th September 2008, Dawson News achieved revenue of £116 million under these contracts. This compares to

> total revenues for Dawson News of £690 million on which it made operating profits of £10.1 million in the last financial year.
>
> The Board and the senior management of Dawson News are currently undertaking a detailed review of the implications, including Dawson's legal rights and the profit impact.

Dawson had pointed out the previous month that contracts were coming up for renewal, although there had seemingly been no particular cause for concern at that stage. It is worth remembering, though, that companies heavily dependent on very few contracts are vulnerable.

In this case, Dawson has been warned well in advance of the terminations so it has time to act. However, these contracts account for one sixth of the news distribution business, a hefty chunk to replace.

Checking back

Astute investors would now take the trouble to refer back to check precisely what the interim management statement issued the previous month had said on the matter:

> **Contract negotiations**
>
> A number of contracts with our newspaper publisher and magazine distributor clients fall due for renewal over the next twelve months. The publishing industry has been affected not only by pressure on circulation but also by significant falls in advertising revenue. There will be significant pressure on wholesalers to create value for publishers and distributors during the contract renewal process. A number of other publishers and distributors, whose contracts are not yet due for renewal, have also engaged with wholesalers to negotiate contracts ahead of the scheduled renewal dates to provide certainty of supply chain arrangements and pricing. Dawson News is proactively engaged in discussions and negotiations with publishers and distributors, the outcome of which will emerge over the next few months. We believe the financial effects of the new contracts will be limited in the current year.

This apparently innocuous indication of routine contract negotiations now takes on a much more sinister appearance. There are several contracts coming up, so more could be lost; the contracts are, in some cases, being reviewed well in advance, leaving ample time for publishers to switch distributors without disruption to supplies; publishers are losing revenue and are therefore desperate to screw cheaper deals out of the distributors, so even if contracts are retained they will be less lucrative.

The point that these negotiations will not affect the current financial year is of little consolation. Losing contracts would have an immediate impact only if they were cancelled early. But these contracts normally run for several years, so the impact over the long term will be lasting as there will be no immediate opportunity to win them back.

Furthermore, if Dawson cannot cling onto the deals it will face the prospect of slimming down the distribution side, with redundancy payments. Some costs, such as depots, will be fixed.

Fears for the future

Worries over the contract renewals had already pushed the shares down from 80p to 50p in the two months before news of the lost magazine distribution sent them spiralling down to 28p.

Figure 12.2: Dawson Holdings

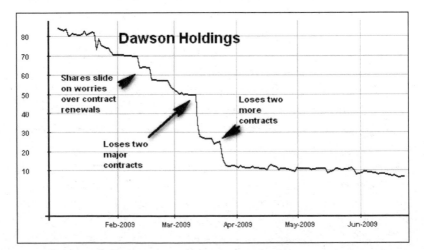

Such fears were justified because, within two weeks of losing the magazine contracts, Dawson was forced to admit the following:

Contracts renewal process

We have now been advised that Comag, another client in the magazine distribution sector, and Associated Newspapers, a client in the newspaper distribution sector, will not be renewing their contracts with Dawson News when they expire in December 2010 and October 2010 respectively. In our last financial year, the revenue attributable to the Comag contracts was £55 million and that for Associated Newspapers was £84 million.

The Board and the senior management of Dawson News are currently undertaking a detailed review of the implications of those decisions, including Dawson's legal rights and the profit implications. The contracts have over eighteen months to run, thus enabling Dawson to initiate contingency plans in part mitigation of the long-term financial impact.

Time to tot up. That makes a total of £255 million a year lost out of revenue at the news division of £690 million.

Dawson also has operations in book selling and marketing but news distribution is by far the largest part of the business. Group turnover was around £775 million in each of the previous two financial years to 30th September so the contracts lost account for one third of total income.

The shares promptly plunged to only 17p.

How are rivals affected?

Where contracts are won or lost, it is worth considering the effects on rivals in the same sector.

Are lost contracts scrapped altogether, in which case no-one gains, or have they passed to another company? Have gains been made at someone else's expense or has new business been created?

In this case newspapers and magazines will still need to be distributed around the country so rivals such as Smiths News, which was split off from retailer WHSmith in 2000, and Menzies Distribution, part of John Menzies, must be gaining. However, they will have had to undercut Dawson to grab the business so their profits will be squeezed, a fact that is reflected in a slide in the share price at Menzies since the start of the year.

Smiths News was the big gainer. Having slid from 80p to 46p over three months, it recovered all the lost ground within a fortnight. Here's the reason:

Major Contract Wins

Smiths News, the UK's leading wholesaler of newspapers and magazines, is pleased to announce it has successfully negotiated new five year contracts with magazine distributors Frontline and Seymour commencing in April 2010. Frontline and Seymour have a combined 40% market share of magazine distribution in the UK.

The contracts have a combined wholesale sales value of approximately £288m per annum and will increase Smiths News' revenues by circa £84m per annum from April 2010. This reinforces Smiths News' position as the UK market leader.

Smiths News' market share of Frontline and Seymour titles will increase from 39% to 55%. The additional territories won will overlap with all but one of the News International territories that were secured last year. In addition, the new contracts expand Smiths News' network by a further seven territories, providing an additional platform for future growth.

Soon followed by:

Major Contract Wins

Smiths News has successfully negotiated new five year contracts with newspaper publisher Associated Newspapers and magazine distributor COMAG. These contracts have a combined wholesale sales value of circa £350m per annum.

The new contract with Associated Newspapers will be effective from November 2010 and will generate an annualised increase in sales revenue of circa £65m.

The new contract with COMAG will be effective from January 2011 and will generate an annualised increase in sales revenue of circa £35m.

As we suspected, the revenue from these contracts is substantially lower than that previously enjoyed by Dawson, so unless Smiths can operate on lower costs – which is possible to some extent as it is a larger organisation and can use its existing network – the profits will be correspondingly lower.

It's a deal

Companies frequently announce specific deals that may or may not be significant. Many are routine contract signings or agreements to supply new customers.

Generally they are positive but one feels that they are announced purely to err on the side of caution – better to make an announcement now rather than have the regulator chase you up later – or to reflect a rosy glow around management.

These announcements rarely affect the company's share price but it is always worthwhile for shareholders to cast a critical eye over them in case they are out of the ordinary.

Case study: Aero Inventory

Look at this seemingly innocuous statement from Aero Inventory, an internet-based supplier of aircraft parts:

Stock Sale

In order to position itself to take on further new business Aero Inventory has completed the sale of a significant quantity of consumable aircraft parts to Air Canada. The consideration received by Aero Inventory for this material is in the form of Bills of Exchange with a face value of approximately US$100 million, maturing in just less than one year. Aero Inventory intends to discount the Bills for cash to provide additional liquidity to facilitate new business. The sale also represents a significant step towards achieving the Company's twin objectives of improving stock turn and releasing cash from inventory.

Notice how this is presented in a positive light as being a prelude to higher sales. 'Positioning the company to take on further business' is the kind of phrase that companies love to trot out but it is not the same thing as actually winning new business.

Still, the sale of 'a significant quantity' of goods must be good news, mustn't it?

Not so. For a start, we do not know how many parts have been sold, nor do we know how much Aero Inventory paid for them or hoped to sell them at. These goods could well have been sold at a loss to get rid of them or in a desperate attempt to raise cash.

This suspicion is reinforced by the fact that the 'consideration' or payment was made in bills of exchange, pieces of paper that are in effect IOUs due to be paid nearly a year hence. Air Canada presumably does not have the cash to pay immediately so there is always the risk, however slight, of default.

But Aero needs the cash now so it proposes to sell the bills of exchange for less than face value – the difference being effectively the rate of interest that any financial institution requires to forgo its cash for best part of 12 months plus the risk of default by Air Canada.

Aero aims to improve 'stock turn' – in other words to shift the aircraft parts faster rather than have them sitting in its warehouse – and to free up cash from inventory, which effectively is saying the same thing.

Points to ponder

There are two points to ponder:

1. Has Aero been dilatory in controlling the amount of stock it holds?

2. How short of cash is it?

The second question was to some extent answered by the next part of the announcement:

> **Share Placing**
>
> Aero Inventory has also considered it appropriate in the current business climate to supplement the cash to be generated by the sale to Air Canada with a placing of new ordinary shares. Aero Inventory has today raised approximately £11.9 million, before expenses, through a placing with certain existing shareholders of 4,762,680 new shares at a price of 250p per share. The shares placed represent approximately 10 per cent of the Company's existing issued share capital.

The placing price was at a discount to the prevailing share price of 275.75p. However, management remained optimistic and shareholders should at this point have considered whether concerns were overstated.

Figure 12.3: Aero

Aero's shares had already fallen from a peak of 720p in November 2007, the decline reflecting the soaring crude oil price and its effects on aviation, but they picked up to 279p that day on this assurance:

Current Trading

Demand from existing contracts continues to be resilient although it would be unrealistic to expect it to remain entirely unaffected by the global economic slowdown. Current trading is in line with management expectations and Aero Inventory is seeing unprecedented new business opportunities with progress being made in a number of new contract negotiations, in particular with one major airline.

The important point is that existing contracts are likely to shrink while new contracts are pious hopes rather than done deals. While it is encouraging that several new contracts are being chased, much seems to depend on one major potential customer and in any case negotiating new contracts can take time.

In the event, a cautious approach proved justified. When results were released the following month Aero Inventory was forced to admit that negotiations with the major airline had collapsed because they could not agree terms.

Although Aero reported sharply higher sales and profits, its shares promptly fell 35p to 170p, a drop of 17%, because of the lost contract. The importance of this contract could be seen from the fact that the company said it was reconsidering the sale of the bills of exchange from Air Canada. Clearly it no longer needed the cash to finance new contracts.

AIM and nominated advisers

Companies whose shares are quoted on AIM must have a nominated adviser, or *nomad* as they are popularly called. Nomads are financial advisers approved by and registered with the London Stock Exchange. They also often act as the company's stock broker.

Because the rules covering a quotation on AIM are generally less strict than on the main board, nomads are required to see that their clients play fair, issuing accounts, calling annual meetings, keeping the stock market informed of developments and so on.

Occasionally a company may decide it wants a change of adviser. Possibly the company has grown in size and feels that its nomad is more at home advising smaller companies. A company will rarely ditch its nomad unless it has a replacement lined up, since companies without a nomad are automatically suspended on AIM.

At other times the nomad may ditch the company. This is unusual, as the nomad loses the fees it is charging, and probably indicates that the nomad is not satisfied that the company is complying fully with AIM rules. It is the nomad rather than the company that gets into hot water with the stock exchange if rules are broken.

Sometimes a company and its nomad simply fall out and both sides feel that a parting of the ways is best all round.

A change of nomad is, on the whole, a negative sign. Where a new nomad is appointed immediately, then probably no harm is done. It is worth checking for any obvious reasons for the change, although notices rarely explain, as in this case from round-the-world yacht racing organiser Clipper Ventures:

> **Change of Nominated Adviser and Broker**
>
> Clipper Ventures is pleased to announce the appointment of HB Corporate as the Company's Nominated Adviser and Broker, with immediate effect.

On this occasion there was nothing sinister behind the announcement, although it would have helped if Clipper had been more specific. In this case Clipper was one of about 30 companies using Teathers as its nomad. Teathers was stripped of its nomad status when its parent company went into administration.

Milestone payments

Small pharmaceutical companies depend heavily on what are known as milestone payments. The receipt of one is good news.

Developing new drugs is highly expensive and time-consuming. Many fail in the early stages of trials. Even those that eventually succeed through three phases of testing, starting with animals and moving on to humans, absorb costs but produce no revenue until they are in production.

Large pharmas, such and GlaxoSmithKline or AstraZenaca, may well have the financial resources to see a potential drug through from start to finish. Because a number of drugs will be in the pipeline at any one stage, there is likely to be the occasional blockbuster on the way to compensate for the many failures.

However, small drug development companies sometimes emerge to pursue a particularly promising drug. The drawback is that if the drug fails then the company is up the creek. Even if the first two phases bring encouraging test results, it may be necessary to go back to shareholders to survive until revenue starts to flow.

To get round this problem, small pharmas often strike a deal with their larger brethren, who will fund research by putting up payments in stages in return for a licence to market the drug, either worldwide or in specific geographic areas.

Each payment is triggered when the drug passes an agreed milestone in development.

While this arrangement sacrifices some income from future sales, it brings in welcome cash now and a larger company may in any case have more success using its proven marketing skills and contacts.

Case study: GW Pharmaceuticals

Here is one example from GW Pharmaceuticals:

GW Pharmaceuticals has received confirmation from its licensing partner, Laboratorios Almirall, that it will pay to GW a milestone payment of £8 million. GW will receive the payment within the next few weeks.

Under the GW-Almirall contract, this milestone payment became due in the event that GW obtained positive results in its recent Sativex Multiple Sclerosis Spasticity Phase III trial and, in addition, Almirall considered that the data was sufficiently positive to include a country within their licensed territory (Europe excluding UK) as part of the resultant Sativex regulatory submission. Following their review of the complete data from the positive Phase III trial announced on 11th March, Almirall have now confirmed their positive opinion of the data and that they wish to include Spain in the forthcoming regulatory submission.

GW has one product, Sativex, a cannabis-based drug with the potential to relieve symptoms of multiple sclerosis and cancer where other drugs are ineffective. Perhaps conscious of the controversy over the use of cannabis as a recreational drug, medical authorities in the UK have been reluctant to sanction its use, although it has been approved in Canada, where it is marketed by Bayer, and one region in Spain.

This has brought in welcome cash but GW is naturally anxious to maximise revenue and has struck a deal with Almirall to market Sativex in Continental Europe if regulatory approval can be obtained. The £8 million milestone payment was triggered by successful Phase III trials. This is the final phase of testing to see if the drug actually works, so things are starting to look hopeful.

Figure 12.4: GW Pharmaceuticals

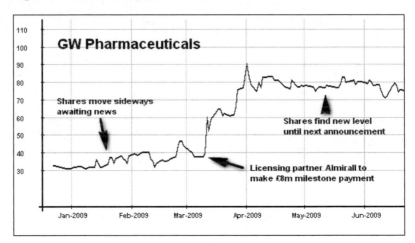

GW shares had an erratic ride after peaking above 150p at the start of 2005 as hopes for Sativex were raised and dashed. They dipped below 30p several times in late 2008 but the promising Phase III results followed by the milestone payment from Almirall sent them shooting up from 38p to 90p in the space of three weeks.

Share issues

Companies sometimes buy back their own shares on the stock market. This was quite a fad in the boom years when profitable companies became awash with cash and didn't know what to do with it. Taking over other companies was not always an option, either because valuations were so high or because no suitable takeover target was available.

The theory was that buying in shares would help to support the share price, so it was particularly popular among companies that had seen their share price fall.

Shares held in treasury

Usually shares bought back by companies are cancelled but not always, as this announcement from software developer Misys shows:

> Misys transferred to participants in its employee share scheme 10,000 ordinary shares at a price of £nil per share. The shares were all formerly held as Treasury shares.
>
> Following the above transfer of shares out of Treasury, Misys plc holds a total of 47,601,385 ordinary shares in Treasury. The total number of ordinary shares in issue (excluding Treasury shares) is 546,982,794.

Shares in treasury are held in abeyance by the company. They can be reissued at any time, either by being sold on the stock market, used to buy another company or, as in this case, transferred into the staff bonus scheme.

Once reissued, these shares will have the same status as all other shares and the holders will be entitled to any dividends paid.

Misys has an unusually large number of shares held in treasury, equal to 8.7% of the issued capital. If these were sold in the market to raise cash they would dampen any rise in the Misys share price.

On the other hand, they could be handy if Misys wanted to make a share placing or issue shares as part payment for any future acquisition.

Delisting

When a company decides to give up its stock market quote it is often bad news, though there may be a silver lining.

You invested in the company because you thought you would get a decent return on your money and you would always have the opportunity to get out if you changed your mind or needed the cash. Now, perhaps quite suddenly, you face the prospect of being locked into a private company with no ready market for the shares and having little or no say in the company.

It is important, as always, to read the company statement to see precisely what is happening and why. The reasons most often given for delisting are:

- the cost of maintaining a listing or AIM quote

- thin or virtually non-existent trading in the shares

- a failure of the share price to reflect the financial performance or prospects of the company

- the company is unlikely to wish to raise further cash

This is all very well but what about the shareholders who do, after all, own the company, which is supposed to be run by the executives on behalf, and for the mutual benefit, of all shareholders:

- the share price will immediately fall on the stock exchange because the company is now unattractive to other investors

- directors will no longer be obliged to comply with stock exchange standards

- there will be no need for the company to pay a dividend to keep shareholders happy

- there will almost certainly be a controlling shareholder, leaving minority shareholders defenceless

- there may be no mechanism for selling shares after they have been delisted

Because the implications for shareholders are potentially so serious, the London Stock Exchange insists that there must be a 75% vote in favour of delisting rather than a simple majority. However, it is quite likely that one shareholder, or a small number of people acting together, have the required 75% and can force the delisting through.

There is no requirement on the controlling interests to offer to buy out the minority shareholders, although they may do so in the interests of goodwill, possible at a comparatively low price.

Case Study: Metnor

Metnor is a property and building specialist that describes itself as a one-stop shop for companies looking to relocate or expand their business. It employs experts in property, construction and engineering mainly for healthcare, student accommodation, leisure and retailing.

Based in Newcastle-upon-Tyne, it was founded by the chief executive Stephen Rankin's father as a contractor in the marine industry but sensibly it diversified as shipbuilding declined and it was floated on the stock market as a galvanising company in 1998. Again it found itself in a declining industry and again it diversified.

The sale of Metnor Galvanizing finally ended its connection with heavy engineering. However, the AIM-quoted company failed to capture the imagination of investors and ultimately the company declared:

Proposed Cancellation of AIM Admission & Notice of EGM

Metnor announces that it is seeking Shareholder approval for the cancellation of admission to trading on AIM of its Ordinary Shares.

An Extraordinary General Meeting is being convened at which a resolution which seeks Shareholder approval for the Cancellation will be proposed.

A circular convening the EGM will today be posted to shareholders. Copies of the circular will shortly be available on the Company's website www.metnor.co.uk.

The announcement gave a timetable proposing that trading of the shares on AIM would cease within a month.

Reasons for delisting

It then explained the reasons behind this move, including the fact that on one third of stock market trading days not a single share changed hands:

> Trading volumes in the Company's Ordinary Shares are very low – median daily volume over the past two years on the London Stock Exchange has been less than 4,000 Ordinary Shares per day. In the twelve months to 31 January 2009 there were 85 trading days when no Ordinary Shares were traded on the London Stock Exchange.
>
> Metnor, like many other small AIM companies, has a tightly held register of shareholders and suffers from a lack of liquidity for its Ordinary Shares. The current share register shows that more than 90 per cent of the Company's Ordinary Shares are held by 15 shareholders.
>
> It is unlikely that Metnor will need to raise money through a new share issue or issue new shares in connection with an acquisition and therefore the lack of Ordinary Shares in free float and low trading volumes will continue.
>
> The cost associated with trading on AIM (estimated at more than £150,000 per annum) is disproportionately high and these funds could be better utilised in running the business. The management time, legal and regulatory burden is disproportionate to the benefit.
>
> The group has grown organically and from targeted acquisitions during the last ten years, consistently producing strong profits, and yet the market capitalisation is today lower than when it came to market in 1998.

The directors strongly believed that 'it is no longer in the best interests of the Company or its Shareholders as a whole to maintain admission to trading on AIM of its Ordinary Shares'.

This was, to say the least, contentious. There was no proposal to buy out the minority shareholders. Metnor shares had traded at 40p before the announcement and promptly crashed to 15p. Not much benefit there.

Figure 12.5: Metnor

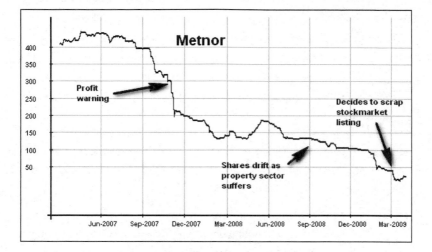

As Rankin held 55.9% and another family member 18.9% it was clear that he was within a whisker of the 75% vote in favour. With shareholders scrambling to get out, he would have no difficulty laying his hands on the other 0.2% cheaply. In any case, it is rare for all shareholders to vote on any issue and the 75% hurdle refers to votes cast at the EGM, not the total share register.

What this means for shareholders

Minority shareholders were left with an unpalatable choice. Sell in the market for what they could get – assuming they could find a buyer – or stick it out in the hope that something would turn up in the long term.

As the statement explained:

> Following the Cancellation, there will be no market facility for dealing in the Ordinary Shares and no price will be publicly quoted for the Ordinary Shares. As such, holdings of Ordinary Shares are unlikely to be capable of sale and will be difficult to value. Furthermore, following Cancellation the financial and other publicly available information required under the AIM Rules will

> be discontinued although the Company intends to continue to provide financial information to its Shareholders via its website.
>
> As and when the Directors believe the Company has the resources to do so, the Company may take advantage of opportunities to buy back its Ordinary Shares. The timing of any purchases cannot be forecast as they would always be dependent upon the circumstances at the time.

So this delisting, supposedly in the interests of shareholders, leaves them with shares that cannot be readily sold and no-one would know what they were worth even if they could be sold.

There is a vague possibility that the minority could be bought out some day but no-one knows when or at what price. In the meantime the company says it will set up a matched bargain facility where anyone wanting to buy or sell shares could be matched up privately but it is hard to see why anyone other than the Rankins would want to buy.

When trading ceases abruptly

At least shareholders get some warning if a company makes a conscious decision to delist. Sometimes trading in shares ceases abruptly.

Troubles at ID Data came to a head in September 2008 when this short announcement was made:

> **Suspension**
>
> The Company has experienced delays in the completion of the audit of its accounts for the year ended 31 March 2008 and no longer expects to be able to publish these accounts by 30 September 2008. Accordingly trading in its shares on AIM has been suspended.

Companies are required to publish audited accounts within six months of their financial year end. Failure to do so means their shares are automatically suspended from trading. This rarely happens on the main board but is an all too frequent event on AIM.

Since most companies have financial year ends on December 31st or March 31st, the most common dates for this type of announcements are July 1st and October 1st. ID Data got in a few days early, quite rightly biting the bullet once it was sure it could not make the deadline.

Simple precaution

Only the doziest investors should be caught out in this situation. It is simple enough to check the financial year ends of any company where you are a shareholder and to look back to find when results were declared in previous years. If the normal date passes without word, start worrying.

The longer the delay in announcing results, the worse they are likely to be. As the six-month deadline approaches, one should fear the worst.

ID has produced accounts but apparently cannot satisfy the auditor. This means either a dispute over an item in the accounts or – more likely and far worse – the accountant is not prepared to certify that the company is a going concern.

Once the shares are suspended they are effectively worthless until the company can redeem itself by producing the accounts and share trading is restored. There is no time limit on how long a suspension can last on the main board, but AIM-quoted companies have only another six months leeway to comply. If the suspension lasts one day longer than that, the shares are automatically delisted.

No prizes for guessing what followed from ID at the end of March:

Cancellation of admission

The board of ID Data regrets to announce that the admission to trading on AIM of the Company's shares will be cancelled with effect from tomorrow.

The Company will contact shareholders, directly, in due course to clarify its financial position.

Any company that needs to 'clarify its financial position' is usually bust, especially if it cannot produce accounts a year after the end of the financial period. There is now no prospect of ever being able to sell the shares.

Restoration of share trading

Sometimes hope does triumph over adversity and a company returns from the dead after its shares have been suspended. If you are in the unfortunate position of getting stuck with untradeable shares, watch out for a brief announcement like this one from X-Phonics, which manages singers and publishes music:

> *Restoration Of Trading On AIM*
>
> **X-PHONICS PLC**
>
> The trading on AIM for the under-mentioned securities was temporarily suspended. The suspension is lifted from 08/04/2009 at 10:30am, the annual audited accounts having been published.

X-Phonics shares had been suspended from trading because it had failed to produce its accounts for the year to 30 September 2008 within the specified six months. Its shares were automatically suspended under AIM rules on 31 March 2009.

At that stage X-Phonics said it expected to put matters right within a couple of weeks and was as good as its word.

However, the company was not out of the woods. A delay in producing results usually indicates bad news and X-Phonics produced another loss accompanied by a gloomy trading statement.

Legal disputes

Court cases are always a bane. They distract management from their jobs, they involve considerable cost and they have an uncertain outlook. Where someone is suing for damages, the potential bill is unlimited, especially if US courts are involved.

Ill feeling engendered between the parties may come back to haunt them. No company wants a reputation for being involved in litigation, whether it is criminal or civil.

Court cases tend to be lengthy affairs; not so much the trial itself but the preparation. For as long as it drags out, companies generally have to set cash aside to cover all eventualities.

Thus, news of the settlement of a court case, even when on seemingly unfavourable terms, can be greeted with relief and a surge in the share price.

Case study: PartyGaming

Take this example from online gambling operator PartyGaming:

Non-Prosecution Agreement Concluded with the US Authorities

The Company has entered into a Non-Prosecution Agreement with the US Attorney's Office for the Southern District of New York.

Under the terms of the Agreement, the USAO will not prosecute PartyGaming or any of its subsidiaries for providing internet gambling services to customers in the US prior to the enactment of the Unlawful Internet Gambling Enforcement Act on 13 October 2006. As part of the agreement, the Company has agreed to pay $105 million in semi-annual instalments over a period ending on 30 September 2012. Such payments will be made from the Group's existing financial resources.

PartyGaming, in common with other providers of facilities to play poker, roulette and the like with strangers, had attempted to avoid US gaming laws by being registered offshore in places such as Antigua or Gibraltar and accepting bets from US citizens, who formed the overwhelming majority of the players.

It is a moot point whether this was illegal. Gambling over the telephone was outlawed in the US long before the internet was thought of, and some

US states argued that the existing law banned internet gambling. Executives of online gambling companies were arrested in transit in the US and it became clear that the companies would be hassled even before a new Act was passed near the end of 2006.

There really was little point in arguing the toss through the courts. PartyGaming had the facilities to meet the imposte. Better to pay $15 million (about £10 million) every six months for the next three and a half years and get on with life.

Figure 12.6: PartyGaming

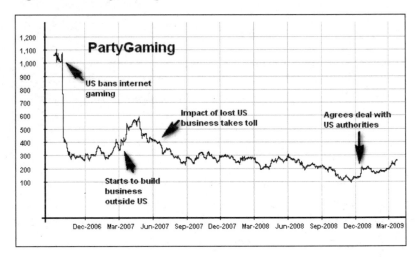

Investors certainly thought so. PartyGaming shares had slumped from above 1000p just before the original storm broke to below 100p as the company struggled to rebuild its operations. On the day the New York case was settled they jumped 32p to 251p.

Going to court

Sometimes companies decide that it is worthwhile pursuing their case through the courts, especially if large sums of money are involved. AIM quoted oil group Sibir Energy decided that a sum in excess of £250 million was well worth the risk:

High Court proceedings

Sibir and two of its subsidiaries have commenced proceedings in the High Court in connection with unauthorised payments.

The proceedings are against former directors, Chalva Tchigirinski and Henry Cameron, Gradison Consultants (a company owned by Mr Tchigirinski) and Derbent Management. Mr Cameron has, as a result of his conduct, been dismissed by the Company with immediate effect.

The total amount claimed by Sibir is currently not less than US$328 million but it is anticipated that the total claims will, in due course, rise to approximately US$400 million.

The High Court has granted a worldwide freezing order under which, pending a full hearing of the claims, Mr Tchigirinski is prevented from disposing of his assets to the extent the value of his remaining assets falls below £250 million. Gradison is prevented from disposing of its assets to the extent the value of its remaining assets falls below £120 million.

Sibir expects that its shares will remain suspended from trading on AIM for the foreseeable future.

The last line carries a sobering warning. Even if there is a successful outcome it will still be some time before shareholders reap any benefits. In the meantime they remain locked into the company with no hope of selling their shares.

The case is against two former directors. Although the statement does not say so, one of them still owns 23.5% of the company and the other ran the company until he was suspended a couple of months earlier.

There is some hope here. Assets worth a total of £370 million have been frozen so there is some hope that Sibir will get its money – assuming, though, that it eventually wins the case, which is not certain. The fact that a High Court judge is prepared to freeze these assets is simply an indication that there is a potential case, not a guarantee of success.

In any case, the High Court ruling may be difficult to enforce abroad. Tchigirinski comes from Russia, where legal niceties do not always match those in the UK.

13.
Scary But Harmless Announcements

While this book encourages shareholders to take proper notice of all announcements, it is important to distinguish between the important and the routine.

Many statements will have a disclaimer like this one on the top (always in capital letters):

> NOT FOR DISTRIBUTION TO ANY UNITED STATES OR ITALIAN PERSON OR TO ANY PERSON RESIDENT AND/OR LOCATED IN THE UNITED STATES OF AMERICA OR THE REPUBLIC OF ITALY

Regulations in other countries may differ from those in the UK and it may be necessary to put on this disclaimer to avoid breaching the rules. Quite why we need to go through the pretence of protecting residents of certain countries – the US and Japan are the main examples – is a matter for the powers that be.

You may feel that all shareholders and potential shareholders are entitled to know what is going on. You may feel that these deprived residents will have no difficulty in finding these statements on the internet. You would be right. The point is that there is nothing sinister, nothing being hidden by the company.

The following is another example of the purely routine, put out to comply with unnecessary red tape:

> **Kingfisher plc – Voting Rights and Capital**
> As at the close of business on 31 March 2009, the Company's issued share capital was 2,360,835,233 ordinary shares.

> Therefore, the total number of shares with voting rights in Kingfisher as at the close of business on 31 March 2009 is 2,360,835,233.
>
> The above figure (2,360,835,233) may be used by shareholders as the denominator for the calculations by which they will determine if they are required to notify their interest in, or a change to their interest in, Kingfisher under the FSA's Disclosure and Transparency Rules.

Just in case you haven't grasped how many shares electrical goods retailer Kingfisher has issued, we get the figure three times. If you wanted to know, you could find it perfectly easily on the company's website.

The importance of the figure is that under the Takeover Code shareholders with more than 3% of any company must declare any purchases or sales of shares in that company.

Forward looking statements

In an attempt to discourage rash forecasts, the US authorities have prompted companies trading in the US or with US shareholders to include a paragraph with the heading 'Forward looking statements' with results, trading updates and other announcements.

This is a particularly pointless exercise and is one of the few parts of company statements that investors can happily ignore.

Company statements inevitably look to the future. As an investor, you want them to. You want to know how the board sees things panning out and how they will react to events.

However, the US requires an often lengthy, cumbersome and quite frightening looking disclaimer that seems designed to scare off investors. In effect, this paragraph seems to imply that no-one has a clue what is going to happen over the coming months and that shareholders invest at their peril.

This is, however, just a catch-all disclaimer to comply with a US law that treats investors as complete idiots. It is detailed to cover all eventualities.

The company can then proceed with whatever statement it is making with impunity.

Here is a typical example, in this case issued by confectionery and soft drinks group Cadbury:

Forward Looking Statements

Except for historical information and discussions contained herein, statements contained in these materials may constitute "forward looking statements" within the meaning of the US Securities Act. Forward looking statements are generally identifiable by the fact that they do not relate only to historical or current facts or by the use of the words "may", "will", "should", "plan", "expect", "anticipate", "estimate", "believe", "intend", "project", "goal" or "target" or the negative of these words or other variations on these words or comparable terminology. Forward looking statements involve a number of known and unknown risks, uncertainties and other factors that could cause our or our industry's actual results, levels of activity, performance or achievements to be materially different from any future results, levels of activity, performance or achievements expressed or implied by such forward looking statements. These forward looking statements are based on numerous assumptions regarding the present and future strategies of each business and the environment in which they will operate in the future. In evaluating forward looking statements, you should consider general economic conditions in the markets in which we operate.

Don't blame Cadbury for this rambling statement of the obvious. It is obliged to bore you with this rubbish.

You are warned: information that does not cover the past refers to the future. If something may or will happen, that is also in the future. So are targets and goals.

If you are surprised to discover that targets are not always met, that policies sometimes fail, that economic circumstances change, then you should not be investing. You should not even be getting out of bed.

A Final Note – On Trading

There is an old stock market adage:

buy on the rumour and sell on the news

Fortunately life is not as simple as that or the market would be a very dull place.

It is true that some short-term investors try to buy ahead of announcements in the hope of taking profits once news is out in the market. Like all bright trading ideas, it works for some of the time but is just as likely to produce a loss as a profit. It all depends on what the announcement says (which is why you have just read this book to gain a greater understanding of the information that companies provide).

It is not within the scope of this book to give a detailed analysis of trading tactics but some general points are worth remembering.

Firstly, if shares run higher before an announcement it is quite likely that there will be profit-taking afterwards. This does offer some scope for buying if shares fall after the announcement but you do still have to assess whether any subsequent price fall is due to profit-taking or because the news is not as positive as expected.

Similarly, if shares have fallen ahead of results then they may bounce higher afterwards, thus offering a better selling opportunity. However, it may simply be that the figures were better than feared and the turn in the share price represents the start of a rally.

On the other hand, if the market underestimated the extent of the good or bad news then the share price chart will simply continue in the same direction.

The important issue is to treat all stock market announcements on merit and decide whether any reaction leaves the shares under- or over-valued.

Secondly, the market tends to react to news instantaneously, especially when announcements are made before the market opens. The scope for getting in at 8am and making a killing is virtually non-existent. It is, on the whole, better to wait to see how the shares settle, unless you feel that the initial market reaction is just plain wrong and you are prepared to back your judgement.

It is true that the market does sometimes change its mind and an early rise in the shares gives way to a fall, or vice versa. This does not usually happen but it is by no means a rarity. It may be that investors start to concentrate on a part of the announcement that was overlooked initially or they decide that, in all the circumstances, the news was not quite as good or as bad as it first seemed.

Thirdly, the situation is potentially different for smaller companies where there is little trading in the shares and one trade can have a disproportionate effect on the share price. If a news announcement provokes trading, it may be that any change in the share price is excessive and thus a buying or selling opportunity presents itself. Do bear in mind, though, that it may be correspondingly difficult to sell out or buy back in at a later date where shares are illiquid and there will be a greater spread between the buying and selling price.

Alternatively, there may be no trading in illiquid shares in response to an announcement so there is a better chance of dealing at a favourable price if you feel the news merits a purchase or sale.

One final point. As noted in Section B, many announcements come out at the same time every year so you can check whether a company that you fancy is due to report soon. Buying just before an announcement offers the scope for a larger reward if figures are better than expected but conversely there is a risk that the news falls short of expectations.

Appendix

Timetables

The table below shows the daily timetable for the UK equity market.

Time	Event
7 am	Trading starts for smaller stocks and AIM
7-8 am	Most of the time sensitive announcements, such as company results and trading statements, are issued
8 am	Trading for larger companies starts
8 am-4.30 pm	London Stock Exchange trading day. Breaking news, such as takeover updates, is issued
4.30 pm	Trading ends
4.30-6.30 pm	News of share buying and selling by company directors is issued
6.30 pm	Stock exchange closes

The table below gives a rough guide to what type of company announcements to expect throughout the year.

Month	What to expect
January	Christmas and New Year trading updates from retailers, supermarkets, pubs, leisure companies
February	Full year results from larger companies with December 31st financial year-end, particularly banks
March	Results continue, mainly smaller companies plus retailers with January 31st year end. Trading statements from companies with March 31st year-end at end of month
April	More first quarter trading statements plus Easter updates from retailers
May	Results from companies with March year-end
June	More March results, first half trading updates at end of month
July	More trading updates, half year results from larger companies including banks
August	June half year results continue
September	Results from retailers, first batch of trading updates for third quarter
October	Third quarter trading updates
November	Half year results to end of September
December	Early indications of Christmas trading from retailers

Index